OVERCOMING
SPIRITUAL
ATTACK

OVERCOMING

SPIRITUAL ATTACK

Ryan LeStrange

CHARISMA
HOUSE

Most CHARISMA HOUSE BOOK GROUP products are available at special quantity discounts for bulk purchase for sales promotions, premiums, fund-raising, and educational needs. For details, write Charisma House Book Group, 600 Rinehart Road, Lake Mary, Florida 32746, or telephone (407) 333-0600.

OVERCOMING SPIRITUAL ATTACK by Ryan LeStrange
Published by Charisma House
Charisma Media/Charisma House Book Group
600 Rinehart Road
Lake Mary, Florida 32746
www.charismahouse.com

Cover design by Vincent Pirozzi
Design Director: Justin Evans

Visit the author's website at www.RyanLeStrange.com.

Library of Congress Cataloging-in-Publication Data:
An application to register this book for cataloging has been submitted to the Library of Congress.
International Standard Book Number: 978-1-62998-741-5
E-book ISBN: 978-1-62998-742-2

While the author has made every effort to provide accurate Internet addresses at the time of publication, neither the publisher nor the author assumes any responsibility for errors or for changes that occur after publication.

First edition

16 17 18 19 20 — 9 8 7 6 5 4 3 2 1
Printed in the United States of America

I dedicate this book to my beautiful wife, Joy LeStrange, who has always been by my side navigating both the rewarding seasons and the challenging seasons. I would not be the man I am without the support and encouragement of such an amazing woman! Joy is the fulfillment of Proverbs 18:22 in my life.

▼▼▼▼▼▼▼▼▼▼▼▼▼▼

Whoever finds a wife finds a good thing, and obtains favor of the LORD.
—PROVERBS 18:22

CONTENTS

ACKNOWLEDGMENTS

▼▼▼▼▼▼▼▼▼▼▼▼▼

I WANT TO THANK my team of radical warriors who forge ahead in the call of God on their lives and ministries. Each person who is connected to me through my various ministries is so valuable and special. I am thankful for every one of you. I also thank Carol Puma and Eileen Hromin for their contribution in editing and reviewing my manuscript. I am blessed to run alongside a whole company of people who are plundering the gates of hell and opening wide the gates of the kingdom.

FOREWORD

▼▼▼▼▼▼▼▼▼▼▼▼▼

M ANY BELIEVERS WALK through life unaware of the evil forces that are working to steal their joy, kill their dreams, and destroy their families. They may never realize how principalities and powers—and garden-variety demons—are influencing their thoughts, lobbing flaming missiles at their relationships, or attacking their bodies with sickness and disease. They often don't connect the demonic dots that would reveal the root of their circumstances and trials or catch on to how the wicked one is working overtime to wreak havoc in their lives.

Although we, as children of God, have authority over the works of darkness, I've learned the hard way that it's difficult to fight a devil you can't see. If you don't know you are under a spiritual attack, then you aren't likely to pick up the sword of the Spirit and engage the enemy in battle. In Nicaragua they have a saying: "A devil exposed is a devil defeated." This means, when you rightly discern the enemy's devices, you can submit yourself to the Word of God, resist the devil, and he will flee (James 4:7). That's why the Apostle Paul told us not to be ignorant of the devil's devices (2 Cor. 2:11).

Thankfully I've learned over the years how to recognize a spiritual attack against my life. But before I was equipped to discern the enemy's fingerprint on my circumstances, in my relationships, or against my mind and body, I plowed through life hoping tomorrow would be better. I felt powerless to change the situations I found myself in. I thought some people were just especially mean-spirited. If I woke up exhausted, I figured it was just due to a restless night. If I got three flu bugs in a row, I reckoned I needed to sleep more, eat better, and take more vitamins.

Of course, not every trial, sickness, or relational issue is the devil's fault. I honestly believe we blame too much on the devil. But many times there is a spiritual aspect to the adverse conditions in which we find ourselves. Consider this portion of Paul's epistle to the church at Ephesus:

> Finally, my brothers, be strong in the Lord and in the power of His might. Put on the whole armor of God that you may be able to stand against the schemes of the devil. For our fight is not against flesh and blood, but against principalities, against powers, against the rulers of the darkness of this world, and against spiritual forces of evil in the heavenly places. Therefore take up the whole armor of God that you may be able to resist in the evil day, and having done all, to stand. Stand therefore, having your waist girded with truth, having put on the breastplate of righteousness, having your feet fitted with the readiness of the gospel of peace, and above all, taking the shield of faith, with which you will be able to extinguish all the fiery arrows of the evil one. Take the helmet of salvation and the sword of the Spirit, which is the word of God.
>
> —EPHESIANS 6:10–17

Spiritual warfare is a reality. The enemy is roaming about like a roaring lion seeking someone to devour (1 Pet. 5:8). When you crossed over from the kingdom of darkness into the kingdom of light—when you accepted Jesus Christ as your Lord and Savior—you effectively enlisted as a soldier in the army of God. You became an enemy of Satan's agenda and a target for the wicked one—especially if you set your heart to do anything at all for Jesus. As a soldier in the army of God, you will face spiritual attacks. The good news is, when you discern the attack against your life, your family, your finances—or anything that belongs to you—you can take authority over the enemy's power in the mighty name of Jesus.

In *Overcoming Spiritual Attack* Ryan LeStrange masterfully outlines how to discern the operation of principalities, powers, rulers of the darkness of this world, and spiritual wickedness against your life. For those new to the concept of spiritual warfare, he expertly explains a spiritual attack and encourages you to resist and fight back with the weapons of your warfare, which are not carnal but mighty through God to the pulling down of strongholds (2 Cor. 10:4).

During his more than twenty years in ministry Ryan has battled many different spirits and emerged victorious in every battle—and collected the spoils of war. In this book he shares relatable, inspiring stories about how he responded to the attacks. Much as a doctor would instruct a patient after diagnosing a physical illness, Ryan equips you through practical insights to discern the signs and symptoms of a spiritual attack—which you may have accepted as natural in origin and common to man. Although what you are experiencing at the hand of the enemy may be common to man (1 Cor. 10:13), it doesn't mean you have to put up with it.

Ryan takes you a step further beyond the diagnosis by revealing three of the most common types of spiritual attacks believers face. This is helpful to new believers and seasoned warriors alike because ultimately the devil doesn't have any new tricks. He's been observing human beings for ages and knows what gets our goat. He understands how to discourage our hearts, weary our souls, and unleash sickness against our bodies.

After Ryan arms you with the information and revelation you need to discern the attacks against your life, he shows you a clear pathway to victory over every demonic force. Ryan walks in a breaker anointing, and I believe you can catch a measure of that anointing by taking hold of the teaching in the latter part of this book. Although the devil will attack again and again over the course of your life, this book will serve as a resource for—and a reminder of—how to battle to breakthroughs in the name of Jesus. *Overcoming Spiritual Attack* is a strategic battle guide for every believer.

—JENNIFER LECLAIRE
SENIOR EDITOR, *CHARISMA* MAGAZINE
DIRECTOR, AWAKENING HOUSE OF PRAYER
COFOUNDER, AWAKENINGTV.COM
AUTHOR, *JEZEBEL'S PUPPETS*

Chapter One

WHAT IS A SPIRITUAL ATTACK?

▼▼▼▼▼▼▼▼▼▼▼▼▼

THERE ARE OCCASIONAL bumps in the road of life, but how do we know the difference between a challenging day, a difficult season, or an actual spiritual attack? How do we open our spiritual eyes to see what is happening and overcome it?

Have you experienced times when you felt like everything that could go wrong was going wrong? You find yourself overwhelmed and bombarded on all fronts. In the midst of multiple crisis situations your mind seems heavy, your body tired, and your spirit dull. You want to pray, and you try to pray, but it seems as though your mouth is filled with chalk and the words fall on hard ground to no avail!

There are fires burning all around you, but you're not sure which one to put out first. It seems hard to believe that so many things could be going wrong at the same time. Part of you wants to ignore what you're facing, part of you wants to fight like a mad warrior, and part of you feels as if you are drowning in a sea of despair. All these descriptions are signs of a spiritual attack. As believers we often live between the tension of two kingdoms:

- *The kingdom of light.* God's kingdom is filled with purpose and destiny for our lives. God, our loving Father, has created such good plans for us! As we walk with Him, the reality of our position in His kingdom becomes clear, as described in Philippians 3:20: "But our citizenship is in heaven, from where also we await for our Savior, the Lord Jesus Christ." We grow wiser concerning spiritual attacks and learn to identify clear victory strategies.

- *The kingdom of darkness.* The devil who leads this world is a dethroned being who really has no authority in our lives. He displays an unusual determination to corrupt and destroy humanity. He is persistent and relentless, continually bombarding the lives of people. This fallen angel named Satan (Luke 10:18) continues to attack, lie, and invade with the intent of crushing God's purposes for our lives.

The reality is that there is an invisible realm all around us. We may live and move in the natural realm, but we all are citizens of the spiritual realm as well. One of the great deceptions the devil uses is convincing people he does not exist. It is an effective weapon because a spiritual attack must be recognized before it can be conquered. Many other individuals are walking around blinded by the lies of the enemy. He has silenced their discernment, blocked their weaponry, and moved in under the cover of darkness.

WE CANNOT IGNORE OUR ENEMY

But, as believers, we are given discernment to know his purposes and schemes (2 Cor. 2:11). It's time for us to open our eyes, discover the real invader, and put him on the run! We cannot adopt the strategy of the ostrich and bury our heads in the sand, somehow hoping that if we just pretend nothing is going on, the attack will cease. This is the warfare plan many misguided Christians embrace. They follow the lead of the ostrich and refuse to acknowledge the existence and work of the devil.

Every time I write, preach, or share any type of message about spiritual warfare, critics raise their voices. "Why are you acknowledging the enemy?" they'll ask. "Why talk about him? Why focus on him?" Other things they say are less kind. They seem to feel as though it is a sin to expound on the strategies of the enemy.

It is a really ridiculous argument to me. Imagine a general with the greatest army and all the military advantages on his side choosing to ignore his enemy because his opponent's weapons and military are inferior. The general decides he will pretend his enemy does not exist. He will hope and pray that nothing happens and will simply try to think positively.

I know what you are thinking: "That is ridiculous!" I agree with you, but that is the approach so many in the church advocate. They want to ignore the devil, pretending he is not there.

This is not a strategy for victory! Jesus did not ignore the works of hell. In fact, He plundered hell and terrorized the devil everywhere He went. There was not a day in Jesus's earthly ministry that He was not harassing the devil. Luke describes one such clash:

He was casting out a demon, and it was mute. When the demon had gone out, the mute man spoke, and the crowd marveled. But some of them said, "He casts out demons through Beelzebub, the ruler of the demons." Others, testing Him, asked Him for a sign from heaven.

But He, knowing their thoughts, said to them, "Every kingdom divided against itself is made desolate. And a house divided against itself falls. If Satan also is divided against himself, how will his kingdom stand?

For you say that I cast out demons through Beelzebub.
Now if I cast out demons by Beelzebub, by whom do
your sons cast them out? Therefore they will be your
judges. But if I cast out demons with the finger of God,
no doubt the kingdom of God has come upon you."

—LUKE 11:14–20

Jesus's ministry brought terror to the courts of hell.
When He showed up, the enemy was not only exposed but
also kicked out. Jesus cast the devil out of the mute man
in Luke 11, and the man's tongue was loosed to speak and
to glorify God. Immediately accusations and persecution
arose against Jesus. This is the same thing we see manifesting all around us today.

When a minister deals with the powers of hell, people
become nervous, afraid, and even offended. These reactions are a manifestation of the kingdom of darkness that
are intended to keep people imprisoned. Jesus revealed
that breaking the power of the enemy and manifesting the
kingdom of God is a revelation of "the finger of God." He
showed that part of His divine authority and nature is to
displace the works of hell.

Some religious people will claim that acknowledging the
existence of spiritual warfare empowers the enemy. He didn't
seem much empowered in the verses of Luke 11! I know there
are those in the church who put too much attention on the
power of the enemy, and I believe you can get out of balance by constantly focusing on evil spirits. The truth is this:
there is a real devil who desires to kill, steal, and destroy. He
has literal plans to execute against the children of God. If we
do not properly understand his mode of operation, he will
launch successful attacks against us.

PREPARATION REQUIRES PRAYER

Even Jesus did not go up against His enemy spiritually unprepared. His life, and therefore His ministry, was built on the bedrock of prayer. Our first and primary pursuit also must be the Father. But notice what Jesus's earthly ministry looked like *after* He came out of prayer and began to travel:

> In the morning, rising up a great while before sunrise, He went out and departed to a solitary place. And there He prayed. Simon and those who were with Him followed Him, and when they found Him, they said to Him, "Everyone is searching for You." He said to them, "Let us go into the nearby towns, that I may preach there also. For that is why I have come." So He preached in their synagogues throughout Galilee and cast out demons.
>
> —MARK 1:35–39

Jesus cast out demons. He tore down the kingdom of darkness and ripped down the false altars. He plowed through the layers of deception, fear, and torment He encountered in people, releasing them from years of captivity.

YOU ARE CALLED FOR A PURPOSE

Satan has no good plans, and he launches no gentle attacks! He is an invading force that desires to steal the blessings of God in your life. It takes relentless faith to counteract his schemes and plunder his gates. We are not called to be passive participants in the kingdom. We are called to be aggressive pursuers of the promises of God. We must be unafraid not only to confront the enemy but also to break his power.

Bishop George Bloomer, founding pastor of Bethel Family Worship Center in Durham, North Carolina, writes in his book *Spiritual Warfare*: "Because we often do not realize the degree of Satan's cunning ingenuity, we are frequently unprepared for the battle we are called to fight against him and his dark forces. Consequently, we end up living defeated lives, thereby not fulfilling the ministry to which God has called us."[1]

Each believer must come to the realization that he is called to be an effective citizen of the kingdom. Every Christian has a purpose. Each of us has a ministry. The problem is that many people do not understand that ministry is all around us. Being a godly father is a ministry. Being a successful mother is a ministry. Being an intercessor is a ministry. Building a thriving business that employs people in the community, funds the gospel, and is led by integrity is a ministry. Working in media to develop quality art and convey a sound message is a ministry.

It is easy to look at those standing on a large stage, sharing the Word of God, as ministers. I certainly honor and appreciate all those who give their lives to preaching and teaching the Word. I believe wholeheartedly in the five ministry gifts and callings (Eph. 4:11–12), but I also know that each believer is commissioned by God to do something of significance in the earth.

Significance cannot and must not be measured by the size of its reach or the accolades of men. Rewards are measured not by the size of your gift or volume of your impact but by the stewardship of your talents. Jesus's parable of the talents (Matt. 25:14–30) shows us that it was the servants' stewardship of what had been entrusted to them that was either commended or rebuked. Their rewards had nothing to do with how great their gifts were.

Spiritual attacks come to knock each believer out of his assigned place. The wicked one and his despicable minions work in concerted effort to bind, hinder, and confuse our sense of purpose. If we do not wake up and properly recognize what is happening, then their plans will prosper and we will miss our reward. We cannot afford to allow that.

A Personal Attack Broken

Once I made a decision that seemed wise but would later turn out to be disastrous. Some new friends had come into my life, and I decided to share a business idea that I had with them. After a series of events we found ourselves in business together in what seemed like a great endeavor. This was such a great opportunity. I was looking for ways to create streams of income in order to be equipped for the ministry. Our fledgling enterprise began to take off, and in no time at all it was rapidly growing. I was so excited!

There was just one problem; I was working with people who began to manifest bad character traits. I had to make some tough decisions. I could either violate my own convictions and breach integrity, or I would deeply offend those with whom I was working. I could not imagine going against my gut in this situation and abandoning the road of character. I had given up so much to step out in faith into the ministry, leaving many comforts behind. Why would I put all that on the line to make somebody else happy? I took a bold stand and was met with fierce resistance.

The process of building a new business turned from joy to sorrow very quickly. There were extreme manifestations of anger and accusation. During several confrontations I was concerned that things were escalating far beyond the boundaries of a normal disagreement. Throughout this conflict it was as though a heavy cloud of grieving and disappointment was hanging over my life. The lingering dispute went beyond just a typical misunderstanding. I found myself questioning all of the decisions that I had made in realigning my life with the purposes of God.

I had relocated as a result of an encounter I had with the voice of the Lord. Had I missed it? Did I not clearly hear from God? Were there really righteous people living in the kingdom, or was everyone living a double standard like these people? Were my prayers effective, and was there a way out? Should I just give up and retreat? These were all weighty questions blazing across my mind. The worst part was that I seemed overwhelmed and foggy. I desperately needed direction, and I needed it fast. I could not go on in this confused and weary state. My joy seemed diminished and my hope depleted.

On Wednesday evening I attended service after work. I had been in a toxic atmosphere all day filled with conflict and uncertainty, not knowing what to do. I have always functioned at my best when I have a clear word and direction from the Lord, but in the midst of this attack those things seemed to be fleeting. As I arrived at the evening meeting, my heart was heavy and my mind overwhelmed. They announced that they were going to do Communion. I love to receive the Lord's Supper, but on this particular occasion I desperately needed a breakthrough. I needed someone to pray over me. I was so hungry to hear from God. It seemed to me that probably that would not happen during a Communion service. The atmosphere is usually focused on receiving the Lord's Supper and not on personal ministry. When it came time, the leaders asked people to line up and come to a table in the front to receive the elements. Two ministers were serving the Communion in the midst of a strong spirit of worship. I walked through the line, and suddenly one of the ministers began to pray at the Communion table and release a prophetic word over me about the attack that I had been under!

The power of God hit me, and I began to weep from deep within. In a moment the weight of the attack was being confronted by the power of God. That day the evil plan of the enemy was broken at the Communion table.

In the days after that prayer the Lord dramatically delivered me from the situation and reversed the attack. There was supernatural restoration on every front, and I was propelled forth in the assignment that God had for me. I learned many valuable lessons during this time of trial that have continued to help me in the years since.

What Is a "Spiritual Attack"?

One lesson is that we cannot overcome a *hidden* adversary. Without properly understanding spiritual attacks, we cannot break free and enjoy the many blessings of the kingdom of God.

We'll begin our study by stating what a spiritual attack is:

> A spiritual attack is a series of events coordinated by the demonic realm to oppress a believer, abort promises, shipwreck faith, and stall out destiny.

The kingdom of darkness aligns accusations, plans, persecution, and circumstances to move the believer outside his destiny and assigned place in God's kingdom. Its evil forces move with great strength and stealth. Their goal is to operate under cover, just as an invading power would when entering the airspace of another nation. They do all they can to remain undetected. "Why?" you may ask. The answer is simple: if the enemy can remain under cover, then his maneuvers can continue. The element of surprise and the art of hidden warfare are key elements of successful battle strategy.

A person under attack feels as though he is living in his

own personal storm. He often wakes up tired and stressed before his feet hit the floor. It is as though a storm cloud is following him from place to place. In one sense this is exactly what is happening because there are actual spirits involved that are buffeting the person on all fronts.

The best picture of a spiritual attack is that of a fierce and sudden cyclone that is released in the peaceful life of a believer. One of the chief differences between a spiritual attack and the average challenges of daily life is the strategic nature of the events and how they unfold. The kingdom of darkness has methodically studied your life in order to painstakingly plan and execute a customized attack designed for maximum impact. A spiritual attack is by no means a random series of events!

Under its intense pressure you begin to question what is going on or whether you have done something to cause your life to spiral out of control. During these conflicting circumstances people around you may begin to manifest anger, hostility, or frustration. Unfortunately the friends and family who typically stand with you in times of crisis may seem to be the very ones who are making things worse. Questions race through your mind: "Can anyone relate to the mess that is taking place in my life? Has anyone else navigated this bumpy road before?"

ZIKLAG WILL REVEAL WHAT'S INSIDE

The Bible describes an incident in which David's enemies successfully executed a secret mission against him and the men who were loyal to him. It was a surprise attack, sudden and devastating, and it struck at everything the men held dear in life:

Now when David and his men came to Ziklag on the third day, the Amalekites had raided the south as far as Ziklag. They had struck Ziklag and burned it with fire. They had taken as captives all the women who were there. They did not kill anyone, but carried them off and went on their way.

David and his men came to the city, and they found it burned with fire, and their wives, their sons, and their daughters taken captive. So David and the people that were with him lifted up their voice and wept until they had no strength in them to weep. Now David's two wives were taken captive, Ahinoam the Jezreelitess and Abigail the wife of Nabal the Carmelite. David was greatly distressed, for the people talked of stoning him, because all the people were bitter in spirit, each over his sons and daughters. But David encouraged himself in the LORD his God.

And David said to Abiathar the priest, the son of Ahimelek, "Please bring the ephod to me." So Abiathar brought the ephod to David. David inquired at the LORD, saying, "Should I pursue after this raiding party? Will I overtake them?"

And He answered him, "Pursue them, for you will surely overtake them and will surely recover all."

—1 SAMUEL 30:1–8

In the span of a moment, as they arrived at Ziklag, these powerful warriors discovered that all they loved and held dear was gone. Their enemies had successfully executed a secret mission, an invasion that resulted in the worst possible outcome for these men. They had been hit hard and decimated on every level.

Examining the meaning of the word *Ziklag* reveals some powerful parallels between the horrendous circumstances of David's men and our own lives. As we look at various opinions and root words associated with Ziklag, a clear picture emerges. Ziklag represents a place of pressure and distress that causes what is on the inside to flow out.[2] The flow comes forth as a result of external pressures being applied.

Many of us have endured our own Ziklags. We have been in places and situations that squeezed us, places that demanded what is locked up deep inside of us to come forth. I remember the words of one of my mentors years ago as he described spiritual attacks. He painted a succinct image, simple yet profound. He said the enemy would put pressure on Christians in times of adversity. He compared the pressure to stepping on a tube of toothpaste and causing the contents to come squishing out.

The weight of pressure reveals what is on the inside. When the pressure is on, what is inside comes out. This is one of the reasons we cannot afford to wait until trouble comes to quote God's promises and stand on His Word. We must meditate on the Word of God, pray in the Spirit, and build ourselves up long before the difficulty arrives. Too many believers are unable to stand against the attacks of the devil because they do not build up their inner man before he attacks.

Ziklag-like attacks are times and places of intense conflict. Ziklag experiences place an almost unbearable amount of pressure on our lives. It is during these experiences that what is inside us comes out and serves as either an instrument of deliverance or a tool that further enslaves us. The result is based entirely on what we have pondered, meditated on, and digested spiritually and emotionally.

THE ENEMY INTENSIFIES THE ATTACK

While David was living through his hellish nightmare, the enemy took the attack to another level. He had already stripped David of his family and robbed him of all his resources. David had been leading his men and doing what he believed was the will of God when everything suddenly went wrong. It was a tormenting situation on all levels. There may not be a more vivid expression in all the Bible of an attack against an individual than the story of David at Ziklag.

David must have had a multitude of questions: "Why did this happen? What did I do wrong? Where is God in the midst of this? What should I do now?" I am positive his mind raced with emotions and thoughts. But all his questions would have to wait because the devil was about to turn up the fire another notch.

In the midst of the nightmare at Ziklag David's own men turned against him. This is one of the most sinister elements of a spiritual attack. The enemy creates chaos and releases horrible accusations causing pain, but then he goes a step further. He attempts to stir up strife and tension in the hearts of your friends, families, and allies. Instead of standing with him, as they should have done, David's men grew divided and rose up against him.

In my years of ministry and leadership experience I have seen similar painful episodes played out in families, ministries, and organizations. It is so sad to watch. Trouble breaks out, and a leader, already in distress, is trying to steer the ministry or organization out of choppy waters when a mutiny suddenly erupts. Or a believer is enduring a grievous spiritual battle, and a trusted friend or family member manifests anger. Why does this happen? It is all part of a dark plan to thwart destiny and destroy the emotional stability of a champion in the making! It is one of the cornerstones of a spiritual attack.

The enemy has no new tricks. He has always used a divide-and-conquer strategy. Let's look at a couple of biblical examples:

"Awake, O sword, against My shepherd and the man
of My association," says the LORD of Hosts. Strike the
shepherd, and the sheep will scatter. I will turn My
hand against the small ones.

—ZECHARIAH 13:7

If the enemy wants to abort the destiny of a ministry or
group of people, his strategy is simple: defeat the leader. To
counter plans of destiny, he begins to release plans of division,
disruption, and disunity. He uses negative thoughts, lying
accusations, and powerful temptations to turn the sheep
against the shepherd. In the midst of that type of attack most
people have no idea what is really going on. Unfortunately
they become puppets in an evil play.

The military has a term for soldiers who accidentally shoot
their fellow officers: "friendly fire." I have heard it said that
in the fog of war things can get messy. When the enemy
is approaching and hearts are pounding and emotions are
stirred, critical mistakes can be made. That natural illus-
tration reveals what also often manifests during a spiritual
conflict.

When the heat is on, soldiers can begin unwittingly to aim
their artillery in the wrong direction. The enemy releases
plans of disorientation so he can shift the battle focus in the
wrong direction and allow his depraved schemes to continue:

If a kingdom is divided against itself, that kingdom
cannot stand. If a house is divided against itself, that
house cannot stand.

—MARK 3:24–25

If the enemy can create havoc in families, division in mar-
riages, and tension among friends, then he can bring defeat.
This is one of the primary aims of a Ziklag attack in your life.
It is sent to divide you from those who are called to inherit

destiny with you. The enemy wants to unleash a firestorm of severed relationships, painful rejections, and broken covenants. He loves to strike and attack when you are down.

DAVID'S KEYS TO VICTORY

Let's examine the keys to victory David employed in the midst of his Ziklag experience. When all hell literally broke loose and his family was gone, his heart was broken, and his most loyal men were turning against him, what did he do?

David turned to the Lord and began to praise and worship Him.

The strongest spiritual position we can have is in the presence of God. Worship lifts us up into the heavenly places. There is a dimension of praise that is like a weapon tearing down the walls of darkness and releasing the glory of the kingdom.

One of the best and most secure places we can run to during a crisis is the place of praise. It is in a time of praise that we go back to previous memories of victory. We lift our voices, giving God exuberant thanks for how He has moved in our lives. We disconnect from our current feelings and circumstances in order to tell God how good He is. We begin to magnify Him with our mouths and give voice to our gratitude for who He is and what He has done in our lives.

Catherine Mullins, a worship leader and instructor with The Ramp ministry in Hamilton, Alabama, says, "When we get our eyes off the battle, we make room for the God of the breakthrough to come and fight for us."[3]

David entered the presence of the Lord.

He turned away from the grievous battle and instead pressed into God's presence. Amid the pressure, pain, and opposition of Ziklag what was inside David came forth. At heart he was a prophet driven to seek intimacy in God's presence, so he was prepared. One key to defeating a spiritual attack is to have already equipped yourself for whatever hell has before hell sends it your way!

David sought God for direction.

A spiritual attack typically sends your mind swirling in a multitude of directions. When you are under attack, you cannot trust your mind and emotions. You must live out of your spirit in those moments. David encouraged himself! He had no other option. His closest allies had turned against him, his family was gone, and it seemed as though the enemy had prevailed. There was no human encourager or counselor to be found in that moment. There was, however, a never-failing, all powerful, victorious warrior who had always led David in the right direction: his God! He turned to the presence of the Lord, silencing his emotions and listening for direction.

David received the word of the Lord, a promise and a directive from God.

His experience serves as an example for us: there is a present promise for every spiritual battle. This is one of the great keys to emerging from an attack with victory—tuning in to the voice of the Lord. You must also tune out all the drama, all the stress, all the lies. This is one of the most challenging things to do in a Ziklag moment. The presence of the Lord is an awesome silencer. If a person breaks through in worship, he will eventually come to a high place of victory.

When God spoke, David arose and obeyed.

That is another key for us: obedience brings the blessing. I remember an attack that a member of my family was going through. The enemy had hit this person in the midst of an adversity, and the atmosphere was very heavy. His pain was pulling on my own heart. I could not stand to see him enduring the hardship he was facing. I began to pray, and all of a sudden God opened up an instruction from His Word. It was a difficult word because it required doing something very contrary to what natural wisdom would say. When I shared what the Lord said, it was as if the light of God's revelation instantly began to move out the darkness. One word of the Lord can release a tremendous victory. David followed God's instruction, recovered all, broke the attack, and was not defeated at Ziklag.

GOD'S PLAN FOR YOU:
ABUNDANT DELIVERANCE

God has a plan of deliverance for you too. You may feel as if you are right in the midst of your own private Ziklag, but there is a prevailing word for you. There is a way out. There is a plan for the abundant deliverance of Jehovah in your life. The adversary is skilled at painting a bleak picture of desolation, but God is the master of the turnaround. His power can bring about divine reversal. His power can bring supernatural recovery. His power can shift the heavens and move the mountains.

It is vital that in the middle of your own personal Ziklag you do not give up. You must get into the presence of God and wait on Him to speak to you. Then get up and run toward the instruction of the Lord. The present adversity is temporary. God can and will bring you out if you obey Him.

The moment you were born again you were translated out of the kingdom of darkness into the kingdom of light. You have been radically reborn and filled with the power of God. Victory was secured for you by the greatest act of love ever recorded in history: a perfect Savior's dying and surrendering Himself for the redemption of all mankind.

For this reason it is possible for you to:

> Be filled with the knowledge of His will in all wisdom
> and spiritual understanding; that you may walk in
> a manner worthy of the Lord, pleasing to all, being
> fruitful in every good work, and increasing in the
> knowledge of God, strengthened with all might
> according to His glorious power, enduring everything
> with perseverance and patience joyfully, giving thanks
> to the Father, who has enabled us to be partakers in
> the inheritance of the saints in light. He has delivered
> us from the power of darkness and has transferred us
> into the kingdom of His dear Son, in whom we have
> redemption through His blood, the forgiveness of sins.
> —COLOSSIANS 1:9–14

We have been provided access to everything heaven has. There is absolutely nothing standing between believers and the One who ransomed them. Every wall has been torn down by the complete work of Jesus at Calvary. The question then arises, "How and why are we attacked?"

The answer is simple: the enemy is persistent; he does not give up.

Though all legal rights to your life were canceled by your decision to become a child of God, the enemy keeps looking for a way into your life, a doorway. He wants to find a foothold. This is his nature. He has been studiously plotting and scheming to take you out. He is not moved by the passing of time; he will wait as long as it takes. He does not give up when the first attempt fails; he keeps coming. He keeps searching, trying to find a way in.

This is why it is vital that we live with our spiritual eyes open. We do not face an imaginary foe. There is a literal enemy who wants to do everything in his power to oppose each of us. But God has given us the ability to see into the spirit realm and be in tune with what is happening behind the scenes. He has provided the counsel of His Word to instruct us in the way we should go and to arm us not only for battle but also for victory. We must discern the attack, seek the face of God, heed His instructions, use our authority, and slam shut every door to the enemy.

Chapter Two

DISCERNING AN ATTACK

▼▼▼▼▼▼▼▼▼▼▼▼▼

W HEN THE ENEMY launches a grievous attack, it is filled with deception. He veils his operations in secrecy. He prefers to operate under the cover of absolute darkness, away from the light of God. He shrouds the attack in mystery, doing all that he can to paralyze your faith by blinding your eyes to the reality of what is actually taking place. Many people succumb to an attack because they don't even realize the strength of the battle.

God's Word is life and truth. It brings divine exposure, victory, and healing. The enemy uses various means to create dull spiritual senses. Part of his scheme is to "naturalize" an attack by convincing us that we are having just a bad day or a difficult season. He plays tricks on our minds by making us think our experience is simply a bad mood, a blue Monday, or a tough break.

I understand—not everything that happens in life is always spiritual in origin. I also realize there are many people right now who are far away from their God-appointed destinies because they live with their spiritual eyes closed. The enemy does not want us to arise in the spirit realm and discern what is actually happening.

A SPIRITUAL ATTACK IS NEVER RANDOM

When we are experiencing a roller-coaster ride of emotions and turbulent occurrences during an attack, we desperately need to have our spiritual eyes fully open. We need all our spiritual senses to be alert, properly interpreting what is taking place. There is often a wicked conductor orchestrating the siege during a series of crises: the enemy. He is the unseen puppet master behind the scenes. He is coordinating all the drama, creating all the tension, and releasing all the lies. He can only lie because there is no truth in him:

> [The devil] was a murderer from the beginning, and does not stand in the truth, because there is no truth in him. When he lies, he speaks from his own nature, for he is a liar and the father of lies.
> —JOHN 8:44

A spiritual attack is never a random set of circumstances. It is something far more sinister. It is the result of evil plans hatched in the hideous corridors of hell, sent in an attempt to take you out. The enemy has marked you for his corrupt schemes. He has maneuvered quietly, hidden in darkness to release fear, oppression, tension, and defeat.

When you recognize what is truly happening, you are empowered to overcome the attack. As long as the enemy flies under the radar, escaping detection, there is zero chance of defeating him. But the believer has been endowed with divine ability and gifts to detect the presence of Satan's kingdom.

Second Peter 2:4 gives us a picture of the comfort zone of demonic forces—darkness: "God did not spare the angels that sinned, but cast them down to hell and delivered them into chains of darkness to be kept for judgment."

Demons live and move in moral and spiritual darkness. They are fallen beings, void of light, truth, and purity. Their rebellion has forced them to live in a dreary realm that is absent of the glorious brilliance of God. They shun light and

prefer to work under the shelter of night. They move with
sinister precision, secretly and quietly maneuvering. Their
plans are hatched in secret and are at the highest level of effi-
ciency when hidden away from the presence of truth. That is
why exposure, recognition, and divine strategy are imperative parts of the battle plan for the believer.

DWELL IN THE SPIRIT AND
DOMINATE THE NATURAL

You will never discern a spiritual attack if your primary point
of reference is the natural realm. It is vital that you move
beyond the sensory realm of sight, touch, and feel. Dwelling
in the realm of the senses and placing it above the spiritual
realm in importance paralyzes faith and blocks revelation.
We are called as believers to dwell in the spiritual realm and
dominate the natural realm.

When we read about the miracles of Jesus and the exploits
of the early church, we get a picture of how we are called to
live. How did Jesus and the disciples perform the exploits
recorded in Scripture? They lived more in the Spirit than in
the natural. They took the unseen realm and brought it into
the seen realm. They lived, moved, and had their being in
the realm of the glory and power of God. They manifested
the kingdom and subdued the carnal.

Living this way is imperative to victory. We were not created to muddle through this journey, bogged down in the
carnal world around us. We are spirit beings created in the
image and likeness of God, called to walk in the supernatural.

The supernatural realm should be a completely normal
place for the believer. It is so sad that people become alarmed,
scared almost, if a minster talks about a vision or heavenly
encounter that has taken place outside a scriptural context.
Yet when we read the Bible, we are reading a supernatural

book. Its pages are filled with mind-blowing miracles, astonishing angelic encounters, unfathomable prophetic declarations, and unexplainable wonders. Therefore the questions for us become: Why do the lives of most Christians today look so different from the lives of those chronicled in the Bible? Why are *we* not experiencing more exploits? Why is the supernatural not occurring in *our* lives regularly?

The answer is found in the absence of the Spirit in most believers' lives. Simply put, we are often so in touch with this earthly realm that we are far removed from the heavenly realm. Our lives should be planted much deeper in the dimension of the Spirit than in the natural: "If we live in the Spirit, let us also walk in the Spirit" (Gal. 5:25).

There is no option to walking in the Spirit if we hope to defeat the enemy in our personal lives. Spiritual attacks will be recognized and conquered in the domain of the spirit. Our spiritual ears must be opened and tuned in to the voice of the Father for us to rise above the plots of hell. One goal of a spiritual attack is to overwhelm the mind and emotions of the person in order to put him completely out of sync with the authority God has freely given him.

YOU NEED EARS THAT HEAR AND EYES THAT SEE

Having spiritual ears that hear the inner voice of the Lord is absolutely key to walking in spiritual discernment. There are promptings and warnings that will come in the inner man, so we must become well acquainted with the sound of the still, small voice of God. Often the whisper of the Lord is occurring in our inner man. Our spirit ears are receiving small instructions that unlock massive breakthroughs. Over time we can train ourselves to tune in, hear, and act on these instructions.

Tuning in begins with embracing a different concept of daily devotion. Many people go into their private prayer times with their lists of requests. This isn't wrong; the Bible tells us that we have not because we ask not (James 4:2), so there is definitely a realm of prayer that includes asking. Moving into deeper levels of communication with God, however, requires the understanding that prayer at its highest is a dialogue, not a monologue.

We must train ourselves to enter the presence of God with an expectation of hearing His voice. In fact, we can learn to live our lives continually tuning in and uncovering revelation knowledge from the Lord that propels us forward on a path of breakthrough. We can develop our understanding of how God speaks and begin to recognize previously undiscovered communication. Hearing and heeding His voice secures our triumph over the enemy.

But for this to happen, our minds must be set on the Spirit and the things of God, not on things that are carnal, worldly, or fleshly:

> To be carnally minded is death, but to be spiritually minded is life and peace, for the carnal mind is hostile toward God, for it is not subject to the law of God, nor indeed can it be, and those who are in the flesh cannot please God. You, however, are not in the flesh but in the Spirit, if indeed the Spirit of God lives in you.
>
> —ROMANS 8:6–9

These verses reinforce the mandate that we have been given as believers to live and move in the spirit. The pathway of victory is one of spiritual progress. We are called to spend time with God in His Word, in prayer, and in worship daily. As we develop strong spiritual disciplines in our lives, we are building a fortress of protection around us. This is certainly not the result of our carnal works but because we are choosing to align ourselves with God. An active spirit life creates a platform of clarity for hearing and receiving the voice of the Lord in our lives.

My spiritual father, Dr. Norvel Hayes, states simply yet profoundly in his book *How to Cast Out Devils* that the enemy searches the inner thought life and emotions of human beings, studying their habits, desires, and frustrations, looking for a way in (Calvary slammed the door on the devil, but he can come in if we open the door to him by our own will):

> The Devil is so deceiving. He knows the lonely spots and the empty spots in a man's life, and he will try to fill it up with something that is phony. And that is the very reason that we should study the writing of Paul in the New Testament, where he says, "Put on the whole armour of God, that you may be able to withstand the wiles of the Devil." (See Ephesians 6:11, 13.) The Devil is here for three reasons, and they are to kill, to steal, and to destroy.[1]

That is what an attack is all about. The enemy is looking to plunder our lives and abort our purpose. He does not come at us with a random attack. He has a custom-made set of circumstances designed to inflict maximum pain and paramount impact.

Spiritual insight and vision enable revelation and discernment. God has given the believer eyes to see: "The hearing ear and the seeing eye, the LORD has made both of them" (Prov. 20:12).

One of the enemy's schemes is to dull our sense of spiritual sight. He desires for us to walk around blindly, void of strategic vision and purpose. But we were never created to live in the dark. We are creatures of light called to dwell amid the radiance of God Himself. This is clearly God's will for us, as Paul wrote in his letter to the Ephesians:

> So that the God of our Lord Jesus Christ, the Father of glory, may give you the Spirit of wisdom and revelation in the knowledge of Him, that the eyes of your understanding may be enlightened, that you may know what is the hope of His calling and what are the riches of the glory of His inheritance among the saints.
>
> —EPHESIANS 1:17–18

God has given us a prophetic spirit to see and know the things that are of Him and the circumstances around us. We have been granted a place at the table of His divine counsel and wisdom. We do not war without vision. Every born-again believer has a set of spiritual eyes.

In these passages from Proverbs and Ephesians we have both Old Testament and New Testament scriptures that speak of inner eyes that are made to see. There is a realm of the prophetic anointing and leading of the Holy Spirit that is visionary in nature. God speaks to us in pictures, dreams, visions, and night visions. We must learn to receive the instructions that the Lord provides to us through our spiritual eyes. I am convinced that God is speaking to His people consistently, but many of them simply fail to recognize His voice.

DISCERN WHAT GOD IS TELLING AND SHOWING YOU

I recently conducted prophetic training for a group of people who had no concept of the voice of the Lord. It was extremely difficult to get them to move beyond their heads and their own ways of thinking and to engage their inner man because they were so dominated by their natural senses.

They thought that if God was to speak to them, then He would do so through a dramatic encounter, a heavenly voice, or a man riding on a white horse. Though all those things can happen, the truth is that many times His voice comes in the form of an inner leading through a picture flashing across our spiritual eyes. It comes so fast that it would be easy to dismiss it as just a thought or an idea.

I can think of many times in my own life in which I have encountered the realm of the spirit through my spiritual eyes. I once had some friends who were associate pastors. One night I fell asleep and began to dream that their lead pastor had stepped down and they had taken over the pastorate. They called me a couple days later and left me a message. Before I even listened to the message, I told my wife I knew why they were calling. She asked me how I knew. I told her I had had a dream about them.

When I talked with my friends, I learned that what I had dreamed was exactly what had happened. God had already gone ahead and prepared the way. The word of the Lord had come to me through the ministry of visions. God has many different ways of speaking to us. The key is learning to recognize that He is speaking.

Just the other day I had a very interesting prophetic encounter. I was praying for a woman, and the Lord told me to pray for her son. I didn't even know she had a son—but God knows all. When I asked her if she had a son, she replied, "Yes!" As I began to pray, I had an inner vision. I saw her son's hands, and I could see the lightning of God (multicolored electricity) in them.

As I was seeing this, I realized that her son had a creative gift in his hands. I began to tell this woman what I was seeing, and she wept. She told me her son is a drummer. The Lord was revealing the purpose of this man's life to me.

He was also giving the mother hope, and together we were interceding for this man's destiny. This all unfolded because of what I saw with my inner eyes. Spiritual sight opens a window to the heavenly realm.

God uses the sight realm of the prophetic anointing in many powerful ways in our lives. In the Old Testament one of the Hebrew words for *prophet, ro'eh,* means "seer."[2] There are many believers who are led by spiritual insight. It is key that you learn to discern this type of leading and activate it in your life.

Learning to properly discern spiritual eyesight will open new channels of the Holy Spirit's leading in your life. There are many different ways God speaks in the visionary realm, such as by pictures, images, and insight through visual expression. Some of the most common visual leadings are:

- *Inner vision:* Almost like a movie reel, this takes place in your inner man. You see something on the inside, but not with your natural eyes.

- *Night vision:* This is a release of heavenly insight that comes in moments when you are between asleep and awake. God suddenly illuminates your understanding. Typically visions are more literal than dreams, which are more symbolic.

- *Open vision:* This is the highest level of visions. Your entire being is caught up in the Spirit, with your natural eyes wide open, and you are transported into the spirit realm to receive a divine message.

- *Trance:* This is viewed by many as controversial because false religions have adopted this practice as a way to receive messages or direction, but plenty of trances are recorded in the Bible. During a trance your body is in a suspended state while you are caught up in the Spirit and receive insight.

• *Prophetic dream:* In this way God speaks in symbols through "dream language" while you are asleep. Most prophetic dreams have to be interpreted to be understood.

These are a few examples of how God communicates with the eyes of the inner man. Any picture, vision, or dream is categorized as visual leading. Gaining knowledge of spiritual eyesight and how it functions creates empowerment.

Faith sees into the realm of the spirit. It looks far beyond the natural realm perceived by the human senses and vigorously sees into the unseen realm. When faith has seen, it then boldly declares what has been discovered. Faith is simply "a spirit of seeing and saying." The "confession" or "proclamation of faith" is one that is made as the inner eyes see into the spirit and are established on truth. "Unshakable faith" is the kind that refuses to bow to the natural realm. It chooses instead to hold fast to the promises of God. Faith is never birthed without insight, without first seeing into the spirit.

LEARN TO DETECT GOD'S PROMPTING

God also speaks to the ears of our spirits. The Bible reveals in 1 Kings 19:11–12 the "still, small voice" of God. Several times in Revelation we are charged to have "ears that hear." This means, conversely, we can have ears that do not hear; ears that are dull of hearing because we are not tuning in, not leaning in to the revelation of heaven. God speaks to us in many ways. We may hear His still, small voice (like an inner conversation), we may hear an inner conversation during which prophetic revelation "bubbles up" inside of us as a dec-laration, or we may hear the audible voice of God with our natural ears.

God can also speak to our spiritual minds. Paul writes in Romans 8:27 about the "mind of the Spirit." The Holy Spirit can give us impressions, God thoughts, or inner knowings and promptings. Revelation can come in many facets. It is vital for us to recognize that God speaks in many ways.

Because these inner impressions, knowings, and prompt-ings often feel small, faint, or not very significant, they are easy to ignore. They are simple yet profound, and they are one of the ways God can lead us. Many times I talk with people who are sincerely seeking answers in a particular area of life. They don't know what they should do and are frus-trated by the lack of clarity. As I dig into their situations, I discover that the Lord is speaking to them, but they are just not recognizing His voice.

I have witnessed so many powerful miracles in my min-istry that began with a slight prompting. I would be min-istering and have just a little tug at my heart to pray for a particular person. I would obey, and it would be as if I tapped a geyser in the spirit!

Spiritual revelation is connected to discernment. *Revelation* is described as "something that is revealed...an enlightening or astonishing disclosure...secret or very sur-prising fact that is made known, an act of making something known: an act of revealing something in an unusually sur-prising way."[3] God has many revelations for you and me as we walk with Him. Nothing catches Him off guard, nor is anything too difficult for Him.

You Were Born to Hear God

Our human spirit is hardwired to hear from God. Simply put, we were born to hear from Him. He has not withheld His information or divine insight from us. It is there for us to discover. We have access to inside information! Why? Because we are spirit beings carrying the spiritual DNA of God inside us. We have full access to divine revelation in the Word and the Spirit:

> For nothing is secret that will not be revealed, nor anything hidden that will not be known and revealed.
>
> —Luke 8:17

God reveals the hidden things. He brings forth clarity. He opens our eyes and ears to receive His instruction. He is not trying to keep us out of the loop. There are things hidden from this world, but they are freely given to the children of God:

> But as it is written, "Eye has not seen, nor ear heard, nor has it entered into the heart of man the things which God has prepared for those who love Him." But God has revealed them to us by His Spirit. For the Spirit searches all things, yes, the deep things of God.
>
> —1 Corinthians 2:9–10

Some preachers have incorrectly expounded on these verses, giving the impression that our understanding is blocked. That is totally false. What God is saying here is that your natural eyes and ears are not qualified to fully grasp the infinite plans He has for your life, but the Spirit of God will illuminate your inner man to understand them. There is no shortage of revelation in heaven. Heaven knows the answer to each and every question. Heaven has the solution to every problem.

You may be saying, "That sounds good, but how does that help me?"

It changes everything! You are a citizen of heaven. You are seated with Jesus in heavenly places, and you have the DNA of the Father inside you. You were born of the Spirit, endued with wisdom, and created to carry insight.

We are empowered to know all things. We do not have to live in a realm of partial revelation. We are ordained to receive illumination and instruction about not only the enemy's plans and tactics but also the Lord's victory strategies for our lives. We should expect the leading of the Holy Spirit in our daily living. Divine interruptions and explosions of insight are to be normal occurrences in the life of a Christian who is following the Holy Spirit.

PROPHETIC MINISTRY: A DIVINE SAFEGUARD

Authentic and healthy prophetic ministry is another layer of protection and revelation for the people of God. It is sad that I must preface that statement with the words *authentic* and *healthy*. The reason I do is that many people miss the mark when it comes to prophetic ministry and Spirit-led living. I have seen many ministers operate in a way that is absolutely contrary to the teaching of Jesus and the government Paul advocated in the New Testament.

Despite that, I am encouraged by the hunger and integrity I see in so many prophetic ministers today. Safe places of prophetic leading and guidance are popping up all over the globe. A safe place is one in which there is a healthy measure of prophetic training, accountability, boundaries, and freedom in the Spirit. I am thrilled that just because things got a little messy in prophetic ministry, people did not give up or check out. If you have had a bad personal experience with prophetic ministry, I would encourage you not to just close yourself off. Simply inspect the fruit before you open yourself up to receive.

I have seen prophetic warnings given to leaders and ministers so many times in order to identify strategies the enemy has planned to use against their ministries. Such warnings can literally be life-saving. The truth is, nothing is coming into or against your life that God doesn't already know about. There is nothing that rises against an ordained word that catches heaven off guard. Prophetic ministries are like powerful trumpets sounding the alarm about the enemy and releasing the call to battle!

The Prophet Isaiah was instructed to actually lift up his voice like a trumpet. God told him to sound the prophetic alarm:

> Cry aloud, do not hold back; lift up your voice like a trumpet, and show My people their transgression and the house of Jacob their sins.
> —ISAIAH 58:1

A trumpet remains silent unless breath flows through it. Without breath it is a cold piece of metal with no distinct sound. The prophetic ministry releases the "wind" and "breath" (*pneuma* in Greek) of God as He speaks through vessels.[4] Authentic prophetic ministry brings great strength, insight, and life-giving revelation. I see the picture of a cold trumpet void of sound as a perfect analogy of the church, and of each of us individually, when we have no prophetic wind in our lives.

In the Bible trumpets were used prophetically in two important ways:

1. *To announce new seasons:* "Blow the trumpet at
   the New Moon, at the full moon on our feast
   day" (Ps. 81:3). Prophetic revelation always
   frames a season shift. Before God does anything
   new in your life, He will begin speaking to you
   about it. He frames each season with a word.

2. *To warn and release a battle cry:* The prophetic
   spirit empowers people for victorious battle. A
   trumpet must issue a clarion call so that people
   clearly hear the prompting and know what to
   do. Being in sync with the word of the Lord will
   arm you for every season and each challenge.

A prophet named Agabus once warned the Apostle Paul
of the impending danger that was awaiting him in Jerusalem
(Acts 21:10–11). True prophetic ministry provides a level of
divine protection and much-needed spiritual awareness.

Prophets and prophetic people can identify false spirits
and announce impending danger. Prophetic ministry
declares words of knowledge and operates in breakthrough
anointing for freedom from attacks. The Apostle Paul was
ministering prophetically in Acts 16:16–18 when he identified
a false spirit in operation and unveiled the hidden darkness
that was trying to thwart the gospel:

> On one occasion, as we went to the place of prayer, a
> servant girl possessed with a spirit of divination met
> us, who brought her masters much profit by fortune-
> telling. She followed Paul and us, shouting, "These men
> are servants of the Most High God, who proclaim to us
> the way of salvation." She did this for many days. But
> becoming greatly troubled, Paul turned to the spirit

and said, "I command you in the name of Jesus Christ
to come out of her." And it came out at that moment.

—ACTS 16:16–18

The demon spirit of divination was hiding under the cover
of darkness, using the girl to follow the men of God around.
The enemy always tries to disrupt and distract. He has no new
tricks. He is doing the same things in the earth today. This
girl was carrying a spirit of divination that represented false
spiritual operations, fortune-telling, and witchcraft. In the
Greek the word for "divination" is *python*.[5] I have preached
many times about the actual spirit of python. Although there
is too much that I could write about it to communicate here,
it can be described as an anti-anointing spirit that constricts
and chokes out life. Without revelation and prophetic insight,
this spirit would have plotted against and hindered the ministry of Paul. He saw what was going on behind the scenes
and brought divine exposure to the enemy's strategy.

The prophetic ministry is a key instrument of revelation
today just as it was in Paul's day. A couple of examples from
my own ministry illustrate this.

A number of years ago when I was preaching in Europe,
a man entered the prayer line. As he reached me and stood
in front of me, the Lord showed me that he was in darkness. I began to loudly and aggressively bind up the darkness. Suddenly he grabbed me around the waist and began
to squeeze. The harder he squeezed, the stronger I prayed,
until heaven suddenly invaded him and he fell to his knees
in tears. I found out later that he was a member of the Mafia
in that nation. A voice had told him to come to the front and
hurt me. The word of the Lord rescued me as I took authority
over the plot of the enemy. Today the man is saved and

delivered, and by the miracle-working power of God he has been released from the Mafia with no negative consequences.

Recently I was preaching in South Florida when I received a word of knowledge about someone with a headache. A young woman came to the front for healing prayer. As she walked forward, I heard the Lord say there was a spirit of fear operating in her life. When I called out the spirit of fear and began to take authority over it, she fell to the floor and began to growl and scratch at the carpet. I prayed aggressively for a period of time, coming against the hold of the enemy. His power was finally broken. The young woman was set free and rose up healed and delivered.

We greatly need prophetic leaders, prophets, prophetic teams, and prophetic teaching and preaching (that unveil revelation) to equip believers and secure our promised victory. The prophetic anointing protects, sees, knows, and guides. Every believer has access to the prophetic spirit simply by advancing his personal relationship with God and having a red-hot prayer life. In addition, God will bring people and ministries into your life to make up the weak points you have and to solidify your faith. He will cause you to be aware of both the potential in a season and the plots against you.

He never releases revelation without providing strategy. When prophetic insight comes forth, it is important to pray and ask God for wisdom. You must know not only the *what* but also the *how* of His strategy. You can petition God and ask Him for a word of wisdom to know what to do with the information He has provided. This leads to a personal prophetic strategy that will empower you to win.

Chapter Three

ATTACK SYMPTOM 1— LACK OF SPIRITUAL PASSION

▼▼▼▼▼▼▼▼▼▼▼▼▼

T HE APOSTLE PAUL told Timothy to fan his personal flame of spiritual passion. This was a strong instruction from a general in the faith to one of his spiritual sons. He was revealing a powerful truth that applies in life and ministry: we must keep the fires of personal revival burning:

> That is why I would remind you to stir up (rekindle the embers of, fan the flame of, and keep burning) the [gracious] gift of God, [the inner fire] that is in you by means of the laying on of my hands [with those of the elders at your ordination].
> —2 TIMOTHY 1:6, AMPC

Each one of us will go through seasons when we feel as if we are in a valley and passion is in short supply. Under the duress of an ongoing attack the level of personal passion often begins to wane. At such times we absolutely must not give up.

There is a personal fire that fuels spiritual progress. That fire is intensified only when the furnace of prayer is tended regularly. You must fully comprehend that part of your job description as a follower of Christ is to be the priest of your personal life. It is your holy obligation to keep adding wood to the fire. It is imperative that you daily enter the place of the burning coals and taste of heaven. If you encounter Jesus in all His glory on a daily basis, your fire will increase and the level of discouragement will decrease.

SPIRITUAL ATTACKS: TWO EARLY WARNING SIGNS

There are two easily identifiable signs to watch for that signal a spiritual attack is under way.

Waning tenacity

This is signaled by a decreasing level of tenacity for the things of God. When Satan's minions are coming against you, your prayer life will seem to be stalled. It feels as though it is almost impossible to touch God in the same way you so easily did in a previous season. This is one of the enemy's tactics. I am convinced that the adversary looses a spirit of heaviness against believers when he places them under a vile siege.

It is important to know that prayer is a progressive journey. I am not saying that each encounter with God will feel the same. There are times when His manifest presence does not seem as tangible, yet in those times He is right there with you. I think the famous poem "Footprints in the Sand" paints a very good picture of the journey. In it the Lord reminds His discouraged follower that during difficult times he is not walking alone; rather, the Lord is carrying him.

All of us, as Christians, have persevered through seasons in our lives when the level of God's presence and the ease with which we pray were tested. This is all a part of our personal growth and development. Yet in those times He is right there, carrying us through.

The kind of void I am referring to is something beyond the normal process. I am talking about an evil plot to stamp out your fire and shut down your spiritual acceleration. In the midst of the intense battle your commitment is tested, and it feels as though it is impossible to push though. Your mind keeps telling you that there is no point to the spiritual labor you are enduring. The inner voice of your reasoning attempts to convince you that you are just going through the motions without any tangible results.

Dulled purpose and passion

A highlight of our spiritual lives is discovering a sense of purpose. An inward passion ignites as destiny is unfolded and vision released. But under the dark cloud of a spiritual attack the senses grow dull, and the passion turns into apathy. If you remain in this condition, it is possible you will head down a road of deception and away from the call that is on your life.

Part of the attack by the spirit of heaviness is a temptation for you to simply buckle under the pressure. Demonic forces are exerting extreme pressure to get you to buckle. You feel the heaviness all around you, and quitting seems like a better option in that moment than enduring. That is all part of hell's plans. One of its chief plots is to get you to withdraw from spiritual disciplines and kingdom service. Simply put, the enemy wants to pollute and halt your prayer life. He then can get you to sit down and put your destiny aside in order to accept a life of spiritual mediocrity and defeat.

The sudden absence of spiritual passion is always like a brightly lit sign pointing to the reality of an attack. One of the markers of the attack is the paralyzing sense that you are spiritually stalled out, like a jet plane that was flying high but suddenly encountered engine failure. You feel an intense sense of heaviness, weariness, and what seems like spiritual exhaustion.

Many times faithful and diligent men and women of God have come to me in meetings and asked for prayer because they felt so drained. They were running their race with fresh breath and much endurance, when suddenly it seemed as though the air was drained from their balloon. In those moments there is the sensation of being under a heavy blanket of spiritual and emotional fatigue. The call to battle is dulled by the sensation of apathy.

FRESH TRUTH TRANSFORMS

It is essential to realize that spiritual *advance* attracts the attention of the enemy. A person who is making progress and is in motion becomes a threat to the kingdom of darkness. Once you have been awakened to particular truths, you are not only called to attention in that area of revelation but also activated for higher levels of service. You exit one elevation in order to rise even higher. It is in this process that there is an intimate provocation. Something deep inside you comes alive, and truth resonates throughout your being.

I have seen people who were in a period of stagnation and then made a change after becoming enlightened to particular truths, only to come under a torrent of evil lies and oppression. The question becomes: Why does this happen? The answer is simple: the enemy is after the radical transformation that naturally develops in your life when truth is revealed to you. The moment illumination occurs in your life, there is a divine realization. It is a key that unlocks the door to revolutionary breakthrough in your life. Jesus described what happens when you see and understand the truth:

> You shall know the truth, and the truth shall set you free.
>
> —JOHN 8:32

Certain bondages exist in the life of a person due to the absence of heavenly perspective. When the truth comes crashing forth like a tsunami of glory, then there is magnificent breakthrough available. The discovery of spiritual truth and the illumination of the Word of God in your personal life catapult you forward in freedom and deliverance. You begin to rise above the tactics of the enemy.

Consistent meditation (digesting, pondering, speaking) on the Word of God brings life-changing insight and victory. As the Word takes root in your mind and emotions, it radically transforms the way you think and live:

> This Book of the Law must not depart from your mouth. Meditate on it day and night so that you may act carefully according to all that is written in it. For then you will make your way successful, and you will be wise.
> —JOSHUA 1:8

When you give yourself over to teaching that illuminates your path, you begin to walk differently. You move into a greater level of kingdom manifestation and power. The enemy hates when a believer steps out of deception into truth. He is angered by the shattering of the chains of lies and oppression.

HOW THE ENEMY COUNTERATTACKS

Satan despises a Christian who is alive and activated, because after a person has been set free, he begins to walk in a higher plane of authority. He is now empowered to manifest and demonstrate the kingdom that ultimately proves the words of the wicked one to be false. His spiritual advancement wreaks havoc on the gates of hell because the believer actually becomes a threat to the devil when he is no longer cowering under the devil's lies.

Satan will then launch a counteroffensive. He must work swiftly and masterfully to persuade the believer to abandon the path he is on and retreat to the familiar bondage. It sounds crazy, but many people have grown so accustomed to limited living that they are actually more comfortable there. Hell knows how to intimidate and deceive the mind in order to keep it bound in a false prison.

As the power play unfolds, the hordes of hell begin strategic movements aimed at aggressively contradicting the truth. One of the first moves is to release a wave of adverse circumstances that directly counter the truth of God's Word in specific areas. For example, a believer comes into revelation about healing and the Bible's promises of wholeness and experiences a breakthrough in his body. The enemy then discharges lying symptoms and spirits of infirmity to shake his faith.

His master scheme is to talk the person out of the promise he has discovered. In order to abort the work of kingdom destiny in the believer's life, the enemy sends literal demonic forces to pluck up what has been planted in the spirit. Jesus described this counterattack in the Gospel of Mark:

> These are those beside the path, where the word is sown. But when they hear, Satan comes immediately and takes away the word which is sown in their hearts.
>
> —Mark 4:15

How long does it take the devil to show up? He comes immediately. He's on the scene right away to sow terrible seeds of doubt and fear. His aim is to put an end to the results of truth in the life of a believer.

Here is the reality you need to understand: when you taste of heavenly things, you simply cannot stay silent, and that is the ultimate threat to hell. Why? Because now you have not only come into breakthrough as a result of revelation, but you have also grown so strong in faith that you become vocal about the truth—and your testimony affects not just your life but the lives of others as well. Revelation produces faith, and faith gets results. Faith manifests explosive kingdom power. This is what hell wants to stop. It wants to stop you from becoming an instrument of freedom in the lives of others. It wants to swoop in and steal that seed.

And don't underestimate the seed. A seed may be a very small thing, but it is packed with potential. The smallest bit of discovery holds vast possibilities for your life and destiny. Many times we do not recognize how powerful a seemingly small nugget of the gospel is. It is so easy to overlook the possibility that a moment of revelation contains. A big break-through is typically the result of a series of what appears to be small steps. The point is that everything begins in the seed stage in our lives. The adversary and his grisly subordinates recognize the DNA of God in the seed and arrive in full force to shut it down.

STAND FIRM IN FAITH

What can you do if you find yourself stuck in neutral and stalled out? How should you respond if your passion has fallen off a cliff? Begin by asking yourself this question: Is there a pulse? This is one of the inquiries that must be made about your spiritual life.

What is a pulse? It's a vital sign of life. The evidence of a spiritual pulse means that you are still alive and active in the Spirit. Your heart is beating with love and adoration for your Savior as you do your best to navigate the course He has established for you.

Passion is a strong feeling of enthusiasm or excitement either for something or about doing something. Where the Holy Spirit is moving, there is supernatural excitement, commitment, and signs of life. We were never created to just go through the spiritual motions; this is an absolute fallacy perpetrated by the forces of hell. So many people are stuck in a rut, passionless, and without a profound sense of urgency or destiny.

I understand that there are times in our spiritual walks when we are holding on to the promise of God; we are living by faith despite the fact that our feelings are not aligned with our faith. What does that mean exactly? It means that there are seasons in which we have obeyed God, endured testing, and believed the promise, yet we are still facing challenges.

What should we do when we find ourselves in such a situation? Though the answer seems simple, it is quite difficult when you are the one facing the challenge. The Apostle Paul gave us precise instructions for this scenario:

> Therefore, put on the complete armor of God, so that you will be able to [successfully] resist and stand your ground in the evil day [of danger], and having done everything [that the crisis demands], to stand firm [in your place, fully prepared, immovable, victorious].
> —EPHESIANS 6:13, AMP

As we grow in both obedience and commitment, the reality is that times of testing will come. It is in these moments that we are forged in the fire. You see, a soldier is never truly tested until he is in an actual fight. Too many Christians give up and quit at the first sign of trouble. One of the first things they do is question what God has already spoken to them. We must develop a deeper root system of faith in our lives.

HOLD FAST TO GOD'S PROMISES

It is imperative that we recognize there will be times when we have prayed, believed, and battled, but the resistance is still there. At those times we have to square up our shoulders, stiffen our backbones, and keep standing! We must resist the devil and tell him, "No!" He will do all he can to intimidate, discourage, and defeat us, but we must dig deep, remind ourselves of the promise, and refuse to cede the ground. We have to declare boldly to the devil, "Satan, it is written!," and then quote the promises of God and refuse to back down. If God said it, then it is yours. Get in your Bible—your promise book—and find all the things He said you can have.

When the wicked one comes in to steal your faith, he will continually rail against you and accuse you. He will do his best to make you feel like a failure. He will point out every negative thought you have had (most of which he initiated). He will tell you your faith will not work and that the promises are not true. He will tell you that you are weak and destined to fail.

It is easy in such times to just give up. You look at all that is going on around you and think, "Maybe I have failed." Sometimes the very fact that you are standing is evidence of God's faithfulness. You need to look at every stone the enemy has hurled in your direction and realize none of them knocked you down for the count. You may have staggered and even stumbled, but bless God, you are back on your feet. You are not dead. It's not over! You have not given up, even after all the enemy has thrown at you. That, in and of itself, is a great victory.

What empowers you to remain standing? It is the promises. It is the power of the Word of God that will make your steps sure. As I have already pointed out, the purpose of the attack is an evil effort to rob you of the truth. Get those promises out and keep them before you. They are your artillery. I wish I could tell you it will always be easy, but that is just not reality. Our faith will be tried at times. The Word promises it: "My brothers, count it all joy when you fall into diverse temptations, knowing that the trying of your faith develops patience" (James 1:2–3).

Challenges and issues will arise in our lives, but we are equipped to persevere through them and come out on the other side. As a matter of fact, tests hold the potential to unlock a level of trust and endurance that propels us into even greater spiritual strength. During times of trial the enemy works overtime to shake us and get us to let go of the promises we have been standing on.

SIGNS THAT SPIRITUAL PASSION IS UNDER ATTACK

People who are spiritually passionate will do things people without passion will not do. I have seen people who have had tremendous encounters with God and began giving themselves to prayer hour after hour. I have been a part of revivals and outpourings that sprang forth in a region and began to draw people to gatherings as God radically altered lives.

You can spot passionate people: they sow, give, pray, and show up. Passionate people don't complain about commitments; they get excited about them because they see them as opportunities. Passionate people pursue. They are devoted to their love relationship with the Lord. Whatever price they must pay for it is not a sacrifice but a privilege to them.

In contrast, when passion is subsiding, people often grow offended. I have learned in my years of ministry that believers who grow dry and weary also become critical. They are cranky and hard to please. Suddenly they don't like the prayer meeting time. They complain about the sound system and the color of the carpet. They get upset with the person who is speaking. The enemy twists it all up while convincing them something really deep has happened that is worthy of their offense. The sad reality is that the person who is most affected by the offense is the offended person. What has upset him is usually not even the real issue. The real issue is the lack of Holy Spirit oil in his life and the loss of his passion. People like this need a personal revival!

Dr. Lester Sumrall, who was a leading deliverance minister in his generation, wrote in his book *Demons: The Answer Book*: "The Christian community must recognize that an aggressive war is being waged on all fronts by unseen and formidable foes. We must exercise dominion over the powers of the spirit world in order to reach the masses of this generation for Christ."[1]

These insightful words pull back the curtain to reveal the truth that so many believers simply do not see: there is a spirit realm all around us. Much of the time the feelings of weariness, inadequacy, and lack of spiritual zeal are the result of an extended assault against the life of a person. The enemy is going after his spiritual heartbeat and trying to choke the life of God out of him. He pollutes his vision, confounds his mind, and hurls negative storms in his direction.

A person without passion has no movement. He is no longer surging ahead. He is not moving under the winds of fresh revelation. He is not operating in a prophetic sense of destiny and spiritual awareness. Stagnation is a great danger! It is one of the by-products of living under siege and being dominated by the powers of hell. If you do not break the attack and rise above it, you will become like a muddy and polluted stream that has no life-giving flow.

The Apostle Paul in his writings about the Christian life compares our journey to walking in the Spirit:

> There is therefore now no condemnation for those who are in Christ Jesus, who walk not according to the flesh, but according to the Spirit.
>
> —ROMANS 8:1

The life of the Spirit is a life in motion. As we obey the Lord, there should be a heavenly thrust that catapults us onward. We should be progressing in our relationship with Him, in our understanding of His ways, and in our obedience to His call. Destiny should be unfolding for us like the story in a well-written manuscript.

In contrast, the image of someone who is no longer moving forward is very different. The term *backslide* paints a picture of someone who became stuck in the quicksand of the enemy's lies. He got bogged down and could no longer move ahead. He eventually gave up and decided to stand still. When he stopped moving on, the pressures of the enemy's aggression began to push him backward. Soon he let go of promises, abandoned hope, and returned to old habits. As the chains of despair ensnared him, expectation gave way to impossibility, faith was replaced with fear, and freedom was abandoned while bondage set in.

PURPOSE UNLOCKS PASSION

Each of us was created with an intended purpose. We were handcrafted by the greatest artist of all time. Every detail of our lives was mapped out and strategically planned. There were absolutely no mistakes or unplanned specifics. We are the delight of our Father. He not only loves us now, but He also loved us before we ever loved Him:

> You brought my inner parts into being; You wove me in my mother's womb. I will praise you, for You made me with fear and wonder; marvelous are Your works, and You know me completely.
> —PSALM 139:13–14

As we each connect with our purpose, we unlock our passion. Discovering the *why* is as important as knowing the *how.* As we walk with God and come to understand His Word, He reveals our unique journey to each of us. He assists us in discovering why we are here and what we can do for Him. He is so good that He has already matched our personalities with our calls. He paid great attention to the details of our lives and ordained each step. When you unlock your purpose, you will dive deep into your passion.

I enjoy listening to people share their unique passions. It is amazing to hear the various dreams people carry in their lives. Each one is so different and has such rich potential. The scientific mind that enjoys the world of calculation, hypothesis, and discovery is absolutely fascinating. The musician who is unconcerned with how something is engineered yet radiates creative juices and sees the world through a series of sounds is amazing. Each personality is very different, yet each of us represents a facet of God's vast nature.

Our lives were never meant to be a series of meaningless events. Our days were ordained to be filled with progressive steps of destiny:

> The steps of a good man are ordered by the LORD, and
> He delights in his way.
> —PSALM 37:23, NKJV

There is the potential for significance in every moment of our lives. Tremendous breakthrough and promotion are usually the result of many small acts of obedience and faithful stewardship. We do not always recognize His handicraft as God is doing it, but His unseen hand is always at work weaving the patchwork of purpose in each of our lives.

DON'T STOP FUELING THE FLAME

Sometimes we grow weary and frustrated because we don't see progression, but destiny is often a journey marked by many seemingly small, insignificant steps. When I look back at the moments in my life when it seemed as if I was far away from my promise, I see that God was still at work in those steps. He was behind the scenes coordinating the details.

Diminished burning passion is clear evidence of the heaviness and stress of a spiritual attack. As the fire dims, a person under attack often lets go of assignments and disciplines that would bring the breakthrough. He begins to feel as though he is just slogging through a monotonous routine with no intended outcome. With each step it feels as though there is no real progress. The goal of the attack is to overwhelm and dull the driving force of purpose. It is a well-coordinated trap intended to put out radical zeal that is meant to burn inside each believer. It is a spiritual mirage that must be recognized as a symptom of spiritual attack.

A person who is under attack experiences a tremendous loss of zeal. There is an inner flame that burns in the spirit man of a red-hot believer. The coordinated efforts of the enemy to bring discouragement and disillusionment are meant to snuff out the inner flame. That flame fuels our tenacity to dive deeper into the things of God and live with intention. When you have an active flame burning inside you, you are not willing to quit. You will get up early and go to bed late to navigate your destiny and seek the Father.

Chapter Four

ATTACK SYMPTOM 2—
EXTREME FRUSTRATION

▼▼▼▼▼▼▼▼▼▼▼▼

W HEN YOU ARE in the midst of a brutal spiritual attack, you will typically find yourself battling frustration and anxiety at a level that is not common in your normal life. Multiple demanding situations will emerge simultaneously, each without a seemingly clear resolution. The enemy uses a variety of storms to oppress the mind and bring great confusion, and the result is that you may feel as though you are often on edge and nervous. If the attack lasts long enough, the pressure it creates, combined with the traffic in your mind, will make it seem as though you are stuck in neutral— or even in reverse, seemingly moving backward in your walk with God. Your natural man will analyze this current state of affairs and decide things are at a breaking point. If this symptom is not dealt with from a strong spiritual perspective, it will give way to a heightened level of frustration in your life.

Frustration is defined as "a feeling of anger or annoyance caused by being unable to do something: the state of being frustrated."[1] I mentioned that multiple demanding situations will emerge. Here's why: The enemy never hits us on a singular front. He always strikes in waves and with a variety of methods at the same time. This is his overwhelm-and-conquer strategy. Strong spiritual warriors recognize his lies, grab hold of the Word of God, and refuse to surrender to the weight of his awful schemes.

EMOTIONS ARE NOT SPIRITUAL LEADINGS

The human mind both processes information and houses our emotions. The spiritual leadings of the Holy Spirit are vastly different from emotions. Unlike emotions, they operate in a realm completely disconnected from the natural realm. They are far deeper than emotions because they are not based in this realm. Rather, they are born of the Spirit of God.

When we are being led by the Holy Spirit, we are receiving revelation and instruction that affect our daily lives. Walking in the Spirit means that rather than responding to our current circumstances by changing course based on what we feel, see, or touch, we dominate our natural surroundings by the power of the kingdom and march ahead based on what God has spoken. Spirit-leadings follow divine guidance and dictate the course. Spirit-leadings do not deal with the natural realm but are born from the eternal and focused on the eternal.

Our feelings, on the other hand, are capable of switching and moving at any given moment. That is why it is imperative that we learn to live from the new nature, which is a spirit being, and not live as fleshly creatures that cower to the dictates of our natural minds and bodies. The Apostle Paul says we must not merely "put off" our former ways of living but also "put on" the new nature:

> But you did not learn about Christ in this manner, if indeed you have heard Him and have been taught by Him, as the truth is in Jesus: that you put off the former way of life in the old nature, which is corrupt according to the deceitful lusts, and be renewed in

the spirit of your mind; and that you put on the new
nature, which was created according to God in righteousness and true holiness.
—EPHESIANS 4:20–24

The old nature, the old way of living, was that of the flesh.
Before we are born again, we are dominated by the desires
of our natural man. The natural man is selfish, looking out
only for what is best for him. The natural man is governed
by a carnal mind that has no connection with God. Series of
ungodly thoughts form imaginations and unlock direction
in our lives that lead us away from the intended course. This
is normal living for a person who is not born again and does
not live a life of the Spirit.

But after we are born again, we have a brand-new nature.
We have the DNA of heaven on the inside of us. The very
kingdom, majesty, and glory of God are in us. The glory of
God is not somewhere far away; it is right in the midst of
our being:

> Even the mystery which has been hidden from past
> ages and generations, but now is revealed to His saints.
> To them God would make known what is the glorious
> riches of this mystery among the nations. It is Christ in
> you, the hope of glory.
> —COLOSSIANS 1:26–27

Our new nature is planted in glory. The essence of who
God is and all that He possesses is not only available to us
but also living inside of us. We have been re-created to look
like our Father, to radiate His nature to others. This may
sound like a peculiar fantasy. It isn't. It is a spiritual reality.
It is a truth that must be accepted and acted on in order to
produce kingdom fruit in our lives. One of the main things
we must learn to do as believers is to fellowship with God

and identify the promises in His Word. That is how we successfully navigate our lives from a position of the new nature and not from the failing pathway of the flesh.

THE EMOTIONAL RESPONSE TO AN ATTACK

Because your natural mind typically experiences a heightened level of tension during an attack, your emotions may rage and contradict what you know to be the promises of God. Enduring a long, ceaseless period of battle makes it very easy to give in to extreme frustration and irritation. These emotions will attempt to dominate your life, creating friction with those around you. This is part of the multipronged strategy of the enemy.

For example, he creates heaviness when you are under a financial battle and then unloads on your mind. As you experience adverse emotions, you find yourself lashing out at loved ones. Before you know it, they are upset with you because of your actions. You want to rectify the situation, but it seems too difficult because of the inner turmoil you are experiencing. The extended period of frustration and irritation should serve as a marker to help you identify what is truly going on around you. These symptoms, combined with the others I am listing, become confirmation that there is a spiritual dynamic to the battle you are facing.

Part of hell's battle plan is to bombard you physically and emotionally in order to move you away from your promise and appointed destiny. Frustration breeds fatigue and emotional weariness. You just want to get out of the fog you feel trapped in.

Often when I pray for a person, and the Lord shows me he is under some type of attack, I see an inner picture of a dark, menacing cloud over his head. I see the violent lightning, the opposing wind, and the stinging hail of adversity that is pouring on him with great force. This is the picture of an ongoing demonic battle. It is as though you have your own horrible storm cloud following you from place to place. And in the spirit realm that is exactly what it is.

The good news is that when God provides revelation, He opens our eyes so that we can arise in authority and break the assignment of hell. When a believer properly identifies what is taking place, he is empowered in the spirit realm to conquer.

Unresolved inner conflict and emotional frustration will give way to behavior that is uncharacteristic for you. You become testy; things that normally would not bring about a negative response from you suddenly do. Situations that typically would not even bother you seem to strike a distressing chord. While your thought life and emotions are under fierce opposition, the enemy is trying to open up another front in the battle for your promise: he is trying to create a demonic vortex from which to suck you up into a higher level of calamity.

STRIFE: DOORWAY FOR THE ENEMY

For example, after you endure a long and bitter season of attack, it becomes much easier to fall prey to strife, a tool the enemy uses to open a door to "every evil work":

> But if you have bitter envying and strife in your hearts, do not boast and do not lie against the truth. This wisdom descends not from above, but is earthly, unspiritual, and devilish. For where there is envying and strife, there is confusion and every evil work.
> —JAMES 3:14–16

I have seen pastors blast their staff members, acting in a way not at all normal to them because they were extremely frustrated. I have prayed with married couples who were at a crisis point with great doubts about their relationship. When we'd get down to the bottom of the issue, it would be frustration, not their love and commitment for each other, that had them on the rocks. A frustrated person will do and see things in a way that is out of character for them.

I learned about the powerful effects of strife and division a number of years ago when a ministry I was leading was under attack. One person kept ignoring my instructions and the principles of leadership that our team had laid out. We kept gracefully attempting to make a course correction, but over a long period of time the situation continued to deteriorate.

As with most of these types of issues, this one finally came to a head. I was traveling out of town for some much-needed rest and relaxation when this particular person once again created a great conflict. My cell phone was ringing off the hook, and it was obvious that the enemy was at work. I had been dealing with the same thing for so long that I found myself extremely disheartened by the entire saga. As I sat there asking for wisdom, the Father spoke to me clearly. He told me He was not able to bless our ministry at the level that I had been asking Him to. I was completely stunned by this revelation—particularly as an answer to a leadership challenge. What was He saying? I began to implore Him for greater details. Why was the blessing being held up? What did this have to do with my current leadership battle? What was the wisdom of the Lord in this matter?

His answers to my burning questions came in rapid succession and taught me a valuable lesson I have never forgotten. (I so love the wisdom of God!) He told me He was blessing our ministry as much as He could, but that there was a major roadblock. I asked what it was. He said there was open rebellion, and the result of the allowed disregard for order had fueled the release of strife and contention. He began to reveal to me that major strife in a family, marriage, or ministry is like an open door or window inviting the entrance of, not heavenly spiritual influence, but hellish spiritual influence. I was stunned. I certainly knew what the Word of God says in James 3:14–16, but I would have never connected it to the situation I was dealing with.

Heaven's perspective looks so different from ours. I was reacting to a negative challenge in our ministry, but God was revealing to me how to slam the door shut on the enemy and how to open the door to the breakthrough. Revelation often unlocks what has been previously locked up. It is amazing what He can do to change a situation. If believers will embark on a time of seeking in the middle of an attack, He can even cause a river to spring up in the desert:

> See, I will do a new thing, now it shall spring forth; shall you not be aware of it? I will even make a way in the wilderness, and rivers in the desert.
> —ISAIAH 43:19

REVELATION, OBEDIENCE, TENACITY: DIVINE WEAPONS

In the difficult times of wilderness attacks there are powerful revelations and abundant grace to be discovered. A person who is under spiritual assault often isolates and retreats, but the proper attitude should be to advance.

When the Father revealed to me what was happening because of the strife, His words became a gateway for spiritual momentum. Revelation from Him opened my understanding to unlock faith and release promises. I asked the Lord about having a team with varying opinions because it seemed to me that there would always be differences of opinion. Would there then always be a blessing-blocker? He explained to me that men and women would always differ in their thoughts and approaches and that this reality is a healthy aspect of a family, group, or team. He went on to tell me that it is not difference of opinion that opens the door for an evil invasion in a situation like the one I was facing, but the work of strife. Strife empowers a host of evil powers to come in and create havoc.

I quickly moved in obedience to the Lord's words and slammed shut the door of strife and rebellion in our ministry. It was not an easy approach to take. I certainly did it with a heart for those involved and with the love of God. My step of obedience angered some and caused a whole group of successful businesspeople to leave our ministry during that time. It seemed in the natural I had made a foolish decision, but I had partnered with heavenly wisdom!

I made ample room for repentance and grace-filled restoration, but those involved chose another road. The result was that the atmosphere changed, the door to hell was closed, and, despite the adverse response, the blessings of God came forth. I have never forgotten that season or the valuable lessons I learned. I am now much more aware of strife's assignment and the need to do everything in my power to abort its work in my life and ministry.

Bill Johnson, senior leader at Bethel Redding church in Redding, California, writes in his book *The Supernatural Power of a Transformed Mind*: "Why do disease and addiction and all the other tools of the devil continue to torment the human race? It's my conviction that if we knew more about spiritual warfare, we could thwart much of what we see. What's needed to cure the incurable and do the impossible is warfare at a level that we have never experienced."[2]

Bill cites a couple of examples from the New Testament.

One is the story of the blind man who was brought to Jesus with the expectation that he would receive a miracle. Jesus spit in his eyes! (See Mark 8:22–23.) Talk about an unusual healing ministry. I wonder how many people today would get really angry if we prayed for them like that! The deeper truth of this account is that sometimes it takes an uncommon act of obedience to get an uncommon breakthrough.

Jesus then asked the man if he could see. He appeared to have received a partial healing, as he claimed to see men as trees walking. He could identify forms and movements but not faces and colors. Jesus touched him again, and the second time his eyes were fully healed. His vision was made normal (Mark 8:24–25).

The man's wonderful miracle required a second touch from God. In the spirit, persistence is a key that unlocks realms of glory and breaks attacks. Spiritual warfare demands tenacity and endurance.

Your Mind Is a Battleground

We realize tenacity is a significant key to freedom when we consider that the thought patterns of a person hold great authority over the direction of his life: "For as he thinks in his heart, so is he" (Prov. 23:7).

That is why the battle for control of the mind is so intense. A person's life will move in the direction of his deepest thoughts and beliefs. There is an inner belief system that dictates the pathway. Our thoughts are so powerful that if we do not renew our minds and align our thinking with God's Word, we can actually shipwreck plans our Father has for us. Wrong thinking forms a blanket over our lives that acts as a demonic barrier of containment. It keeps us bound and locked out of God's promise. We can sit under powerful revelatory teaching that points the way forward, yet we seem to be stuck in low gear and cannot accelerate. What is the spiritual issue? Is the spirit man not filled with enough power? Is the Word not strong enough to release us?

The answer is our own minds: "For as he thinks in his heart, so is he." Inner belief systems link together to form a cage that keeps us trapped. We have to break free by planting our thoughts in the Word of God and strategically putting the Word before our eyes.

Our core beliefs and imaginations have to take on God's way of thinking. We cannot allow ourselves to remain stuck. We must let the Word of God be like a bright light shining on the dark areas of our thinking that need to change. The mind can become a catalyst for amazing growth and break-through as it submits to God's Word.

Whispers, lies, and accusatory thoughts are continually invading the mind of the person under fire. The enemy will release a negative or fearful thought, then paint a picture of impossibility or defeat. Our mind's eye begins to imagine the outcome and how bad it could be. This is the power of imagination at work but in a negative way. God created our imaginations to see His promise and give our faith a picture of what it has seen. There are faith imaginations in which our minds ponder the wonderful possibilities of God and His promises to us. We must learn how to take authority over the lying mental accusations and negative pictures that try to lodge in our minds. It is part of the battle.

THE POWER OF LOVE

Your mind was not created to live in a state of negativity. As a child of God you were born to walk with God and live as He lives. God is never depressed. He is never worried about how something is going to turn out. Heaven does not hold crisis meetings, trying feverishly to figure out what to do.

Heaven is not concerned about how to pay the light bill. No, heaven is living in fullness in every area because it is ruled by the Creator. All provision is manifest. All healing is manifest; there are no sick people in heaven. There is no tension or strife in heaven. All is well in God's realm.

You may be thinking, "That is just great. But I am not living in heaven!" Well, the truth is, you are called to live much more in heaven's atmosphere than in the earth's:

> Therefore pray in this manner: Our Father who is in heaven, hallowed be Your name. Your kingdom come; Your will be done on earth, as it is in heaven.
> —MATTHEW 6:9–10

You are called to manifest the kingdom of God on earth. His kingdom is a place of deep peace, rich provision, and limitless possibilities.

Powerful deliverance occurs when the unadulterated love of God is revealed in the life of a Christian; you become freed by love and free to love. The love of the Father breaks chains of torment and fear, and your mind becomes absolutely free from fear and bondage:

> There is no fear in love, but perfect love casts out fear, because fear has to do with punishment. Whoever fears is not perfect in love.
> —1 JOHN 4:18

The door to fear and anxiety can be slammed shut by the revelation of the Father's heart and renewal of the mind by the Word of God. A fear-free life is a worry-free life. When the door of fear is slammed shut, the enemy does not have a crack to enter. As the revelation of the Father's love floods your mind, you are released from self-protection and self-sufficiency. You now rely on the Father for everything you need. As your heart grows in trust toward Him, you are not mired in the fears of failure, lack, need, or abandonment. Security grows inside of you as you move away from your own guidance and surrender your life to Him, trusting that He has the best in mind for you.

GOD'S WORD IS THE BEST MEDICINE

The Word of God has a renewing and redeeming power. Just as natural water can wash away the remnants of dirt, so can the water of the Word of God wash stains and pain away:

> That He might sanctify and cleanse it with the washing of water by the word, and that He might present to Himself a glorious church, not having spot, or wrinkle, or any such thing, but that it should be holy and without blemish.
> —EPHESIANS 5:26–27

Many people get trapped in fear, frustration, and anxiety because they do not allow the Word of God to wash over their minds. There is tremendous power and peace available as we meditate in the Word.

Take hold of scriptural promises and place them in your mind's script. It is key to breaking old thought patterns. You must literally take the medicine of God's Word regularly and submit your mind to the mind of Christ. Two things will happen: first, there will be a literal healing as the Word of God washes out all the junk in your natural mind, and second, you will begin to identify and cast down wrong thoughts and thought patterns as you align with God's Word. This process will dramatically alter the direction of your life in a positive way.

The adversary uses extreme frustration, anxiety, and

mental accusation because he understands the power of the human mind. It is the center of thought and logic. It is also the dwelling place of endeavors, dreams, and creativity. He knows that if he can conquer your mind, he can conquer your life. Your mind is where you make the choice of which way you will go. Your spirit can know the proper path, but if your mind is dominated by the carnal realm, then you will move in the opposite direction. If your mind is planted in the Word of God and your spirit man is leading the journey, then you will move in the direction the Father has for you. As your mind is healed, renewed, and freed, then you become truly free. Inner transformation leads to utter transformation.

Chapter Five

ATTACK SYMPTOM 3— CONFUSION ABOUT PURPOSE

▼▼▼▼▼▼▼▼▼▼▼▼▼

O NE OF THE keys to victory in the life of a believer is the discovery and strong grasp of purpose. There is an internal compass that guides each person toward his God-given destiny. A spiritual attack comes to shake the sense of purpose and muddy the waters, thus producing confusion. One of the major goals of the enemy is to launch an attack that will move a person out of divine purpose.

Every life has a declared destiny. The master planner of all the ages has already spoken His plan over every one of us. This is one of the things I really enjoy about the prophetic ministry and anointing; it discovers and unlocks the word that is hovering, waiting to be discovered. When a prophet or prophetic person sees, senses, and declares something, it feels to him as though he is discovering brand-new information. Yet it already existed. There is power in the discovery and declaration. God created the entire known world by declaring, by speaking.

A quick reading of Genesis 1 shows that the phrases "God said…" and "it was so…" are repeated over and over during the creation account. (See Genesis 1.) They reveal that prophetic creativity was operating at its highest level. I believe when each of us is born, there has already been extensive planning and speaking over our lives. Part of our assignment is to embark on the mission of discovery.

DISCOVER YOUR WHY
AND PLAN YOUR HOW

We tap into the mind of God and recognize the *why* in our lives, and by the leading of the Holy Spirit our reason for being becomes clear. The why is the first step. We must unearth our unique potential that exists in our lives. When we have discovered this key, we can then work on the *how*. Every why must have a how. The how is the plan.

Many people have tapped into a sense of purpose and have an idea of why they exist and what they are to do with their time on planet Earth. They may have even discovered some of their gifts. Each purpose has gifts that empower it. The artist who is created to communicate visually is born with a gift to create. The writer who is called to pen stories of faith and affect culture is born with a storytelling mind. He can accurately communicate intricate details in a colorful way to show the reader the exact picture he is painting with words. The entrepreneur who sees life as a series of opportunities and transactions has a grace on him to build, acquire, lead, and steward.

When you observe a person operating in a gift at a high level, it is mind-boggling because he can do something grand; yet what he does and how he does it seem to flow from him effortlessly. This is evidence of the presence of a gift. God never establishes a purpose without a gift.

Properly identifying a purpose will not ensure forward motion, however. There must also be the how, the plan of action. A series of steps must be taken to move toward the identified goal. Many people fall in love with the grand concept of the why but refuse to take on the difficult task of the how. The how is not always fun or glamorous, but it is essential to success.

For many years I have trained various types of ministers

while teaching at Bible colleges and schools of ministry. One of the common issues that arises when a young person embraces a grand call to change the world is that he abandons the disciplined pathway necessary to form his character, refine his soul, and prepare his spirit for the journey ahead. The real truth is that no one arrives at destiny fully prepared. A series of seemingly small and often difficult steps guides us to the place of launching forth. The greatest launches are those that have been well prepared.

The late Dr. Myles Munroe brilliantly communicates the importance of divine destiny in his book *In Pursuit of Purpose*. He writes:

> A lack of purpose and the impending tragedy that results from its absence are found not only in people but in all things. When elements of nature lose their purpose, chaos and destruction are the results. When nations, societies, communities, organizations, friendships, marriages, clubs, churches, countries, or tribes lose their sense of purpose and significance, then confusion, frustration, discouragement, disillusionment, and corporate suicide—whether gradual or instant—reign.
>
> *Purpose is the master of motivation and the mother of commitment.* It is the source of enthusiasm and the womb of perseverance. Purpose gives birth to hope and instills the passion to act. It is the common denominator that gives every creature an element of distinction. This guiding sense of purpose is more than an orientation toward a goal. Rather, it is a deep awareness that a common vision encompasses all life and existence. Without this vision, we can only exist. We feel no passion for living, neither do we have a reason to wake up in the morning.[1]

Each person's destiny is crafted along with a personality, preferences, and gifts to match it. One of the great deceptions of the enemy is that we have to change everything about ourselves in order to live out our purposes. That is a lie from hell. If God wanted someone else who looked differently, thought differently, and acted differently than you, He could have chosen that person. But He chose you for your own hand-picked purpose.

Knowing how threatening purpose can be to him and his evil plans, Satan moves in with cunning, deception, and pressure to prevent it from being fulfilled. He has done this since the very beginning, starting with Adam and Eve:

> Then they heard the sound of the Lord God walking in the garden in the cool of the day, and the man and his wife hid themselves from the presence of the Lord God among the trees of the garden.
> —Genesis 3:8

This verse was written after the fall of man, but it gives keen insight into the relationship between God and man in the garden. Man was one with God in fellowship, dominion, and glory. Man had been created to walk with God. This was—and still is—the highest calling of our lives, to live for the pleasure of our King.

Two Weapons of Attack

Two of the enemy's chief weapons in an attack aimed at moving someone outside of purpose are *mental attacks* and *pressure.*

- *Mental attacks.* The devil attacks the mind and begins to twist thoughts and perspective in order to bring confusion. I have never

seen a single case of spiritual attack in which
the person has not experienced some type of
tormenting confusion. Satan's mental attacks
cause a person to be paralyzed in his thought
life and left bewildered.

- *Pressure.* This tactic is a lead indicator of a
  demonic plot. The kingdom of God is full of
  power and authority—but not pressure. The
  Holy Spirit leads us (Rom. 8:14); He does not
  force us or intimidate us into being obedient.
  Those are tactics of our enemy.

So many times in ministry I have discerned a wrong
motive in a person by the level of pressure that he is exerting.
When a person bombards a leader with his own desires, dem-
onstrating a driving force that lacks patience, an impure
intention is generally present. Any plan of God will with-
stand time, prayer, and scrutiny. But that is not how the
devil operates. He bombards your mind with a false sense of
urgency, driving you toward his objective, which is to bring
destruction.

Satan successfully executed one of the greatest spiritual
attacks in history against Adam and Eve. He deceived them,
confused them, and pressured them before at last convincing
them to believe and act on his lies. Their cooperation hurled
humanity into a chasm of sin and separation that would
require the greatest act of love in history to redeem:

> Now the serpent was more subtle than any beast of the
> field which the LORD God had made. And he said to
> the woman, "Has God said, 'You shall not eat of any
> tree of the garden'?"
> And the woman said to the serpent, "We may eat

of the fruit from the trees of the garden; but from the fruit of the tree which is in the midst of the garden, God has said, 'You will not eat of it, nor will you touch it, or else you will die.'"

Then the serpent said to the woman, "You surely will not die! For God knows that on the day you eat of it your eyes will be opened and you will be like God, knowing good and evil."

When the woman saw that the tree was good for food, that it was pleasing to the eyes and a tree desirable to make one wise, she took of its fruit and ate; and she gave to her husband with her, and he ate. Then the eyes of both were opened, and they knew that they were naked. So they sewed fig leaves together and made coverings for themselves.

—GENESIS 3:1–7

What was the result of Satan's successful attack? He removed Adam and Eve from true purpose. They were meant to walk with God and live in communion with Him. As part of the curse caused by their disobedience, they were relegated to a life of toiling outside the garden. They no longer enjoyed the constant and effortless flow of provision. They lost the supernatural covering that was on them, and their nakedness was revealed. They left the glory they had known and died spiritually.

There is something special about the precious oil of the Holy Spirit. When that powerful oil flows, the impossible instantly becomes possible, the crooked places are made straight, and God's *super* comes on our *natural*. One term the Bible uses to describe the oil of the Holy Spirit on a believer is *the anointing*. When oil is poured out on a life, things are never the same.

Jesus walked in the anointing and went about setting captives free and destroying bondages everywhere He went:

> God anointed Jesus of Nazareth with the Holy Spirit and with power, who went about doing good and healing all who were oppressed by the devil, for God was with Him.
>
> —ACTS 10:38

As believers we are called to live in the overflow of the Holy Spirit. We are called to get in the flow of the Spirit, stay in the flow, and release the flow. As we allow the mighty Holy Spirit to flow through us and out of us, we become instruments in the hands of the master conductor of the ages who aligns us with the symphony of heaven. Each of us is called to allow the rivers of the Spirit's living water to flow from within us (John 7:37–38).

THE ANOINTING: OIL OF PURPOSE

There is a transforming element to the anointing of the Holy Spirit. Some of the most powerful preachers I know are quiet and meek people in private, but when they begin to speak to a group of people and the oil begins to transform, they become as bold as a lion. Over the years that I have been in ministry, I have watched as God's precious anointing has empowered people to do things that in the natural are impossible.

The anointing not only empowers purpose but also reveals it. We see this in Scripture when the Prophet Samuel was sent by the Lord to anoint a king over Israel. He found a shy young man named Saul, and what was the first thing he did? He poured oil on him:

> Then Samuel took a vial of oil and poured it upon his
> head. And he kissed him and said, "Has not the LORD
> anointed you over His inheritance as ruler?...And
> the Spirit of the LORD will come upon you, and you
> will prophesy with them. And you will be turned into
> another man."
>
> —1 SAMUEL 10:1, 6

Every gift and purpose has its own unique oil. Each destiny has a special anointing on it. The anointing is connected
to the purpose on our lives.

As Saul was being anointed by God, he was also changed.
The supernatural power of the Holy Spirit brings divine
metamorphosis. Not only does God call us by His grace, but
He also supplies the power, ability, and transformation to get
the job done. Many believers miss this point: there is power
in purpose.

A believer who is walking in his destiny is satisfied,
excited about life, and moving forward. That does not mean
there will not be struggles. I don't know of any person who
has achieved something great who has not had to overcome
some hurdles. It's all part of the journey. The truth is that
when you are strongly connected to your purpose, you are
constantly unlocking divine ability and flow. You will never
find a time recorded in Scripture when God called a man or
woman to do something and did not also provide oil to get
the job done.

SIDETRACKED FROM PURPOSE

One of the most alarming examples of a powerful biblical leader being sidetracked from his purpose is David
when he had an affair with Bathsheba. We find the story in
2 Samuel 11. David spotted Bathsheba outside bathing one day
and began to lust after her. He ultimately succumbed to the

temptation and had a sexual encounter with her, resulting in her becoming pregnant. In an effort to cover up his mistake, David had her noble husband, Uriah, killed after his plot to deceive Uriah failed. David's sin cost him the life of his child and almost robbed him of his anointing and destiny. It was only after a prophetic rebuke and humble repentance that he was restored.

What was the open door for the sin of this God chaser? How did he become so distracted? Why was he ensnared in such a powerful way by the enemy? I believe the answer to all these questions is found at the beginning of the story:

> In the spring of the year, the time when the kings go out to battle, David sent out Joab and his officers, all of Israel with him. They brought to ruin the Ammonites and besieged Rabbah, but David remained in Jerusalem.
>
> —2 SAMUEL 11:1

David was a king who had risen to prominence because of his military strength. He knew how to lead people into battle and to victory. Yet where was he at the time when kings went to war? He was at home in the palace. He was walking outside his purpose and anointing.

If the enemy can launch mental torment against a person and confuse him about purpose, he can eventually separate him from the life-giving flow of oil. This is his aim. He wants to bombard us with so many onslaughts that the voice of destiny is diminished and the sense of calling grows dim. He wants to remove us from the field of purpose and sideline us in the bleachers, disconnected from the action. This is what happened in David's life, and this is what is happening in the lives of many whose destiny has become clouded under the weight of an attack.

I have seen powerful ministries destroyed because the

leader yielded to an attack and gave up his post. Because confusion, pressure, accusation, and discouragement bring heaviness, a person in the midst of a demonic siege can easily get sidetracked and turned away from his high call. When the enemy separates him from the call of God, he also separates him from the oil on that call. Each of us has an inner oil. As believers, the Holy Spirit lives in us, and we carry the kingdom within us. God's power is inside each of us, but there is something unique and precious that happens in a person's life when he soars on the winds of destiny.

AM I REALLY SUPPOSED TO DO THIS?

Through a number of prophetic encounters the Lord had clearly spoken to me about my call to revival ministry and to contend for an awakening in my generation. My heart longs to see the supernatural and the reality of Jesus demonstrated to people. I could fill many pages with stories of miracles that I have seen in my years of ministry.

Over the last few years there has been a real uptick in the passion on my life for revival. There have been so many times that the Lord has poured out in an uncommon way during my travels. In the midst of some of the greatest moments I have encountered this awful voice. It will come to me right after I just saw multiple deaf ears open and say, "This is crazy. You are crazy! What are you doing? You should just have a nice, normal ministry." I know that this is the voice of the enemy. He is planting seeds of doubt.

The enemy is faithful to his assignment. He keeps sowing the doubt by asking the same question over and over again. I was in Kentucky, ministering in a real strong atmosphere of revival. One of my very close friends came up to me and shared her encounter with this evil voice. She is a woman minister who has been set ablaze with a passion for revival.

She was recounting stories to me of lying on the floor of her church all alone in intercession crying out for her region. As she stepped forward into what God was asking of her, she would begin to hear the accusations of the enemy. She described a voice that sounded just like the one that I have encountered. This voice was saying the same exact things to her! I told her, "Well, you just described my life!" She asked, "Really?" "Absolutely," I replied.

In an attempt to confuse me about my purpose, the enemy kept releasing these accusations. I dug my heels in and decided that I would not bow to those lies. In fact, I have come to view his attacks as a confirmation that I am on the right track.

GOD'S PURPOSE FOR YOU DOESN'T CHANGE

In recognizing the vast nature of God, we realize that He created each of us as unique expressions of His nature. Every life holds the potential to reveal a part of God Himself. Each child of God is invited to exit low-level living, which focuses only on selfish wants and needs. We have received a summons to operate in a higher realm. We are empowered to navigate life from a perspective of eternity; therefore we must accept the reality that we were born with explosive intention. There has never been a single person—not one—created without a distinct call on his or her life.

One of the great adventures of walking with God is navigating the pathway to purpose and uncovering the richness of His vast plans. In the realm of the Spirit there are no boundaries of time. As unfathomable as it is to our natural mind, God sees the end from the beginning:

Declaring the end from the beginning, and from ancient times the things that are not yet done, saying, "My counsel shall stand, and I will do all My good pleasure."

—Isaiah 46:10

He has established each person's direction and already declared his expected end:

For I know the plans that I have for you, says the LORD, plans for peace and not for evil, to give you a future and a hope.

—Jeremiah 29:11

So many times in the midst of a challenging season we begin to question the word of the Lord over our lives. We look around ourselves, with very limited vision, and declare that we are not moving forward. Based on momentary adversity, we succumb to the deception and believe that an eternal purpose and spiritual declaration has somehow been affected. The reality is that when God declares something, that spoken word stands beyond the boundaries of time. It is an eternal promise that must be received and acted on in order for it to fully manifest.

Far too many people have let go of key words and promises that were declared over them. In the heat of battle they just gave up and irrationally decided that God must have changed His mind! The reality is that God does not change His mind about His will for you, but *you* can choose to abandon course and delay progress.

DON'T LET GO OF YOUR DESTINY!

Pressuring you to quit is one of the major thrusts of the adversary while bombarding your life. He is trying to move you away from both your purpose and your potential. He wants to get you off the potter's wheel and cement your feet in the bonds of doubt. If he can stop your destiny, then he will have derailed a God-sized dream that carries eternal weight and glory.

This is one of the things we absolutely must understand when the enemy comes with his pressure, accusation, and lies: our obedience to God's plan holds rewards and consequences that are eternal. The minister who has been called by God to lead people in the way of salvation and then gets bombarded by the fiery darts of hell has a choice to make. Will he stand in the knowledge of what God has already said, or will he just give up? If that person gives up, he abandons a set of eternal rewards and also vacates a spiritual post that has tremendous impact on the lives of others. Viewing our present challenge through the lens of eternity empowers us to stand firm.

When the Lord revealed your purpose to you, giving you prophetic promises and words that point to what is to come, your purpose was sealed. God declared those things over you, and He meant them. He is not wavering now in His desires for your life. Rather, the adversary is trying to move you outside of faith and create a wavering spirit within you that will shipwreck your destiny and keep you from receiving the promise. You must not succumb to the temptation to abandon ship; you must dig deep and stir up the promises within you. Wavering faith will not receive the answer:

> If any of you lacks wisdom, let him ask of God, who gives to all men liberally and without criticism, and it will be given to him. But let him ask in faith, without wavering. For he who wavers is like a wave of the sea, driven and tossed with the wind. Let not that man

think that he will receive anything from the Lord. A
double-minded man is unstable in all his ways.

—JAMES 1:5–8

The man who asks in faith and keeps believing will receive.
The man who asks and then doubts, then asks again and
believes, then falls back into doubt will not receive. The devil
wants to create a wavering mentality in your life. He wants to
pry your hands off the promise and shift your mind over into
continual questioning. Then he wants to fill your mouth with
complaints in an attempt to destroy your answer. Recognize
his lies and tell him, "No!" Do not give in to his vile schemes
and allow yourself to have a wavering mind that goes back
and forth without receiving the answer. Everything God has
already said to you and about you is true! The prophetic proclamations over your life are not only true but also alive and
active. You must partner those words with faith and tenacity.
Instead of speaking complaints, you must keep declaring the
words of the Lord and refusing to give in to the pressure of
the enemy.

Let your mouth align with the declaration of heaven over
your life. Focus your heart and mind clearly on what the
Lord has said. Speak the promise. Command the storm. Stir
up the prophetic potential that exists in your life. Do not
allow yourself to be tossed in the sea amid a storm of confusion and doubt.

SEEK WISE COUNSEL

When you identify the confusion that's attempting to attack
your mind and cloud your realization of purpose, you will
have uncovered the reality of the attack against you. In addition to getting out your prophetic promises and reminding
yourself of them, you may need to seek the input of someone

who is outside the immediate line of fire you are experiencing. This is why spiritual relationships are so vital and life-giving. There are times when we need an anointed person to release the word of the Lord over us and break the heaviness.

When you are in the intensity of the battle, it is easy to seek out voices of comfort that will identify with your pain but not call you up higher. Doing this is a key mistake. One reason people are often offended by a prophetic anointing is that prophets do not seek to comfort the soul but to charge the spirit. There is a time and a place to bring comfort, but there is also a time to release fire and challenge a person to rise:

> Where there is no counsel, the people fall; but in the multitude of counselors there is safety.
>
> —PROVERBS 11:14

Wise voices are like a safety net in your life. The experience and perspective in them grant you a level of wisdom that's above what you currently have to navigate through the enemy's storm. Not only that, but if the counsel is coming from godly people, then there is an endowment of divine ability and power working through them that can break hell's grip on your thoughts. Seeking counsel from key advisers in a time of crisis is a wise battle strategy.

Don't listen only to the voices that sympathize with your struggle and empower your pain; listen to those that are speaking to you from the high places. They are calling you up. They may charge you to let go of some things. They may challenge your thinking. They may even offend you—for a moment—but ultimately they are seeking to empower you for the road ahead.

Chapter Six

ATTACK SYMPTOM 4—
LACK OF PEACE

▼▼▼▼▼▼▼▼▼▼▼▼▼

THE KINGDOM OF God is filled with peace. One of the ways we can properly discern the internal leading of the Holy Spirit is with the presence of deep, inward peace. There is a realm of supernatural peace that is promised by God but must be accessed by faith. Peace is part of our covenant assurance as believers:

> For unto us a child is born, unto us a son is given, and the government shall be upon his shoulder. And his name shall be called Wonderful Counselor, Mighty God, Eternal Father, Prince of Peace.
> —ISAIAH 9:6

Jesus is referred to in this passage as the "Prince of Peace." We do not belong to a kingdom that is filled with confusion. We are established in a position of glorious and absolute peace. God doesn't move in tension, strife, division, or torment. We were radically delivered from the grip of hell, and that includes the atmosphere of hell.

We have been handcrafted to live in a place of purity, unity, and power that is free from the dictates and emotional upheaval of the evil one. The enemy loves to create tension, drama, and confusion. One of his favorite tactics is to move in with pressure and then create questions about direction.

He wants to accuse and attack in an effort to rob abiding peace and purpose and to destroy destiny.

In her book *Let God Fight Your Battles* Joyce Meyer writes: "Do you know what the Bible means when it says that we are more than conquerors through Jesus Christ [Romans 8:37]? I believe it means we do not have to live in fear. Before a battle even begins, we have already been told that we will win it. We know the outcome—we can enter God's rest knowing we will come through it victoriously."[1]

There is a heavenly rest that comes when we are firmly planted in God's provision for our lives. Worry goes right out the door when the Word of God is the dominant force in our lives. We begin to walk in the realization that Jesus has already provided the victory. It is not a future promise but a past-tense work and present help!

As we trust His word and lay hold of our covenant with Him, we experience a release from strain and toil. Man was not created to live in an atmosphere filled with anxiety over how and when things will work out. That is the result of the curse. We have been delivered from the power of the curse. We have been radically re-created as new creatures who can walk with God. He is at work in every detail of our lives. There is an inward power available to us as we tap into the Word of God and take authority over the negative seeds Satan has sown in our minds:

> Be anxious for nothing, but in everything, by prayer and supplication with gratitude, make your requests known to God. And the peace of God, which surpasses all understanding, will protect your hearts and minds through Christ Jesus.
> —Philippians 4:6–7

This passage of Scripture begins with a strong charge to pray. If we camp out in the presence of God, reminding ourselves of His precious promises, then we gain access to a peace that is beyond natural comprehension. A strong prayer life coupled with daily commitment to the presence of God is the bedrock of our walk with Him.

PEACE SPRINGS FROM RELATIONSHIP

So many believers come into God's inner chambers only when they are in a time of desperate need. Don't get me wrong—He is your Father and is right there ready to help in your time of need. But He ultimately wants to have a relationship with you. It was for this reason that Jesus was sent to the earth: to reconcile us to the Father:

> All this is from God, who has reconciled us to Himself through Jesus Christ and has given to us the ministry of reconciliation, that is, that God was in Christ reconciling the world to Himself, not counting their sins against them, and has entrusted to us the message of reconciliation.
> —2 CORINTHIANS 5:18–19

To *reconcile* means "to restore friendship or harmony; settle, resolve <*reconcile* differences>."[2] harmonize, to bring into agreement. Jesus died to reconcile us to God, to bring us back to our intended position as sons and daughters of God. He did not die so we could have just an occasional, casual relationship with Him. *No.* He died so we could walk with Him on a continual basis.

Our relationship with God is planted in regular fellowship with Him. That is what prayer is: communion with God. We enter His presence, pouring out our hearts before Him. We express our longing and gratitude for all He has done.

We stand on His Word and thank Him and praise Him for His promises over our lives. We pray in the Spirit and in our known language.

We not only talk to God in prayer, but we also listen for His voice, waiting to hear Him talking to us as well. We must be quick to recognize His voice and honor Him when He is speaking to us. Prayer is not intended to be one-sided communication. The mark of successful prayer is encountering God on some level. You come before Him to be with Him.

"HAPPINESS" IS FLEETING

Understanding God's divine peace requires recognizing that there is a difference between godly peace and momentary happiness. In our society we describe ourselves as "happy" when things are going right. If we have a victory on the job or in business, we feel happy. If something good happens in our families we experience emotions that accompany happiness. But happiness is a shallow and short-lived feeling. Many people in today's world make terrible decisions based on emotional happiness. Marriages end in divorce without any good reason because a spouse decides that he no longer feels "happy." No consideration is given for the family that's at stake, the well-being of the children, or the honor of the Scriptures. People make extreme moves and life decisions based on how they feel at a given moment.

This shallow perception of happiness is dangerous not only because it is fleeting but also because it is very deceptive. It has become the mission statement of a selfish generation determined to live for its own reckless desires. When we watch leading television shows that deal with huge life changes and lasting consequences for many people, we see counsel given that often says to put your personal happiness first. Unfortunately it is a message that has entered the church with a vengeance and dominated the thinking of many shallow Christians. They actually believe their entire existence is to be about making themselves happy. But it is a belief that is opposite to what Jesus preached:

> Greater love has no man than this: that a man lay down his life for his friends.
>
> —JOHN 15:13

Your relationship with Jesus will require some tough choices. There are things that your flesh wants to do that the Bible says you are not to do. There will be times when you will be asked to lay down your life for another person, as in marriage. This type of personal sacrifice is one of the works of Jesus. Regarding marriage, Christ invites a husband to love his wife as He loves the church. What does that mean? It means in order to love, protect, and serve the one with whom you have entered into covenant, there must be a death to personal agenda. The reality is, if you are walking in the Spirit, then you reap tremendous reward and a momentary death to a desire of the flesh yields a phenomenal harvest:

> For the one who sows to his own flesh will from the flesh reap corruption, but the one who sows to the Spirit will from the Spirit reap eternal life.
>
> —GALATIANS 6:8

Doing things God's way releases multiple levels of rewards. When I was called into the ministry as a teenager and began to serve Jesus, I thought I was giving up so much. I was marked as a "Nazirite" (see Numbers 6:1–21) and said no to many things my peers were doing. Now, when I look at the condition of my life, my mind, and my family, I am so thankful for that narrow road I chose. I could have whined and complained about how unfair it was and how I was missing out on so much. But that is simply not true. Was it tough at times? Sure, but the rewards far outweighed the price.

The Apostle Paul experienced a daily surrender: "I affirm, by the boasting in you which I have in Christ Jesus our Lord, I die daily" (1 Cor. 15:31). He was not trying to obtain temporary emotional happiness but an enduring life in Jesus. He understood, as we need to, that a life established in the will of God will produce much fruit. Jesus affirms this in John 15:5: "I am the vine, you are the branches. He who remains in Me, and I in him, bears much fruit." This type of surrender will require a denial of the natural man and his fleshly appetites in order to give life to the spirit man and his divine nature. The price is small when compared with the benefits.

There is a peace available to us that's of far greater value than the positive emotions that may come because of our present surroundings. Present happiness can come and go based on what is happening in our lives at any given moment. That is not the case with the peace of God.

PEACE THAT PASSES UNDERSTANDING

When Paul declares in Philippians 4 that there is a peace that passes our natural understanding, the word he uses for "understanding" refers to the mind or intellect.[3] Paul is speaking of our faculties and the ability to reason. He is saying there is a realm of peace that is disconnected from our natural minds, that there is a holy conviction of the reality of the Word of God that produces an immovable inner strength.

For example, a doctor looks at a believer who is walking in healing peace and declares an awful diagnosis. That person seems totally at rest, announcing that he knows he is healed, and he refuses to be moved from that belief. He has an inner calm that is not connected with what is manifesting in his outside circumstances; it is based on the measure of the kingdom he carries inside.

This is the peace that guards our hearts and minds. The Greek word for "heart" used in these verses is *kardia*, which means the inner life, "the affective center of our being."[4] Supernatural peace can protect your inner thought life and emotions from veering dangerously off course. When your center of reason and inner being are fully established in the principles of God's Word and not moved by adversity, your steps are secure.

This is the place Paul is guiding us into. It is a completely uncommon walk that is readily available to the man or woman who taps into the revelation of prayer and faith. In the Amplified Bible (Classic Edition) translation of Colossians 3:15, we are given a vivid picture of the role of peace in the leading and direction of a believer's life:

> And let the peace (soul harmony which comes) from Christ rule (act as umpire continually) in your hearts [deciding and settling with finality all questions that arise in your minds, in that peaceful state] to which as [members of Christ's] one body you were also called [to live]. And be thankful (appreciative), [giving praise to God always].

In this translation peace is compared to the umpire in an athletic event. What is the role of the umpire? He is a moderator, arbitrator, and judge appointed to monitor the athletes, enforce the rules, and make sure the event is fairly played.

Inner peace plays a similar role in the life of a Christian. It is one of the methods God uses to lead His children. Many times I have advised people to tune out their natural emotions in order to think, ponder, and pray over a decision—and then afterward check their level of peace. "Think about going right, and then ponder it," I'll advise. "What do you sense deep down on the inside?" Then I'll ask them to think, ponder, and meditate on going left, asking again what they sense deep down. When there is not a clear dream, prophetic word, or other dramatic leading that is drawing an individual to make a specific choice, peace can be an easy indicator of the will of God.

Another way to view the role of peace is as a weather buoy in the deep ocean. The buoy monitors the conditions of the sea, alerting when something is happening that could pose danger. Inner peace is like a spiritual buoy surveilling the water line of the Spirit in your life and keeping you on course. You can follow after deep, abiding peace. It is a measuring instrument confirming in your heart and life the will of God.

PERSONAL PEACE IS VITAL

Spiritual attacks are aimed at robbing your peace and placing your soul in a torrent of negative emotions. This is why the enemy works overtime to place fear, torment, and anxiety on you during a spiritual attack. The attack against your level of personal peace is yet another effort from the forces of darkness to move you outside of your rightful position as a child of God. It is meant to distract and deceive you concerning the promises of God, and ultimately to arrest your journey into destiny.

The reality of the vital importance of personal peace and its connection to your assignment is further revealed in the description of the armor of God that Paul gives us in Ephesians 6:10–18. In verse 15 he tells us to have our feet "fitted with the readiness of the gospel of peace."

Taking a deeper look at the Greek word for "shod" clarifies the picture. Verse 15 is literally telling us that we are to "bind under" and "bind on" the supernatural peace of God on our feet.[5] Each piece of armor described in the longer passage serves a well-defined purpose. So the question becomes, why is it so critical to have the peace of God on our feet? Peace seems like something we would put on our minds. What is the significance of the particular insight that our feet need to be shod with peace?

I believe that in this scripture feet represent "assignment" and "dominion." For example, God told Joshua, "I have given you every place that the sole of your foot shall tread, as I said to Moses" (Josh. 1:3). Joshua was sent to occupy lands and territories. Wherever his feet went, there was a spirit of dominion and conquering, as he boldly obeyed the promise and went after the reward.

In every assignment God gives, there will be both tests and attacks. I have endured seasons when I knew I was exactly where I was supposed to be, doing exactly what I was supposed to do, yet there were tremendous resistance and battles.

The Apostle Paul faced strong defiance throughout his ministry exploits. Everywhere he went to take the power of God and release revival, he faced a fight. The forces of hell acted in direct opposition to the apostolic assignment he carried.

These forces absolutely did not want to see the kingdom advanced, lives forever changed, churches established, and souls saved. Demonic forces opposed him on every front, working as hard as they could to shut down his progress and drag him out of obedience. Whenever the reach of his ministry and its effectiveness expanded, religious men and women would rise against him and attack him, not just spiritually but verbally and physically as well. He faced a fierce, mighty, and ongoing battle, but Paul stayed in the peace of God; he wasn't moved. He marched on despite it all.

WHY THE ENEMY TARGETS PEACE

How do you endure an attack without being moved? What do you do when it feels as though the wind has been knocked out of you? How do you react after experiencing what appears to be a crushing defeat?

You must move beyond the emotions circling your mind and tap into your spirit man, releasing inner strength. There is an unwavering strength in the realm of the spirit. You have to dig deep and stand firm in your born-again spirit man. The seas of life can be storming all around you, but when you walk in the Spirit and discern His path, there is divine peace and presence to hold you in the will of God.

Typically when a person is experiencing a protracted and burdensome spiritual attack, his mind swirls with gloomy thoughts of defeat and his emotions are under extreme pressure. As the demonic crushing continues, he senses a loss of peace.

Your peace is one of the chief targets of the enemy. He understands that if he can cause a lack of peace and throw your emotions into a cyclone of pain, then he may be able to move you outside of your assigned place. He also knows that you are increasingly weakened as you are moved farther away from your purpose. He knows you will become disillusioned, confused, and discouraged when you get away from your call. His siege against your emotions is directed at your spiritual feet and at doing all that he can to remove the peace from them so that he can get you to abandon your post.

This is the exact strategy he used with the great Old Testament warrior Samson. He lured that mighty man of God through his greatest weakness—his lust for beautiful women. He drew him into a relationship with the wrong person—the woman Delilah—who was outside Samson's call as a Nazirite, a man consecrated to God. Then the evil spirit of seduction cast a deep slumber upon him. His soul became numb, and his spiritual senses were dulled. He succumbed to the slow, downhill motion of bondage and disobedience.

Delilah pressed him daily. His soul (mind, emotions) became vexed. He was not at rest. She pushed and pushed with relentless force and wicked intent. The enemy was using her to take out a champion. Finally, after her many attempts to seduce him, Samson revealed the secret of his heart to her and was taken captive by the Philistines. His hair was cut and his strength stolen. That is a picture of the wicked one's plan: to remove you from the place of obedience and power, rob the anointing from your life, and shackle you with defeat.

Samson spent his final days without vision. He was blinded, bound, and afflicted. He could no longer operate in the strength and anointing of God. How did he arrive at this place of defeat? He did not properly discern and resist the menacing ploys of the enemy. He allowed himself to be seduced by the deceptive lure of temporary pleasure. This is the way the enemy binds so many: he dangles a carrot of disobedience in front of them that has the power to draw their attention away from consecration and personal obedience and drag their feet off the narrow path.

He targets personal peace because he aims to take out personal destiny. When your feet are firmly established on the will of God and cemented in deep spiritual peace, you are immovable. You begin to manifest your kingdom assignment. You take your divine position. You enjoy navigating your spiritual destiny. The onslaught of attacks against peace are designed to bring fierce agony until you give up and forfeit destiny.

One of my first positions in full-time ministry was as an administrator of a Bible college. It was a powerful school of ministry that brought forth life-changing teaching on faith, purpose, and deliverance. The atmosphere was rich with the power of God. I still remember our times of prayer, teaching, impartation, and revival. On so many days the glory of God would roll in and transform the students.

It was a school of the Spirit. God would send us broken students who desperately needed healing and freedom. They would charge in with the absolute conviction that they were in the right place at the right time. As the school year would unfold, commitment would be tested. I can remember so many days when my heart was broken over a student in the midst of an attack who would leave the school, never completing his courses. Even though it has been quite a few years, I can see some of their faces as I write these words.

What was it that robbed their sense of commitment and pushed them out of their assigned places? The short answer is simple: it was a spiritual attack. An unholy assault was waged against the heart (inner being, center, core) and mind of each one. There was a barrage of negative thoughts hurled at their intellects. The enemy kept the pressure up. He made his voice seem louder than any other, and they failed to recognize what was happening. Amid the anger, frustration, disappointment, and fear they felt, they decided the easiest pathway was to abandon course. I am sure that with many of them, if we could dig deeper, we would find that the enemy had come after their peace and gotten their feet to move in the wrong direction.

An Attack Against
Destiny in Central America

I still remember when I was in Bible college and the Lord had a conversation with me about the call upon my life. There were several things that He revealed to me during this encounter. One of the things that He told me was that

I was going to take His power to the nations. He unfolded a mandate to me for global ministry. This mandate has propelled me into many nations sharing the gospel. I have been so blessed to travel all over the world. It all began with one simple encounter!

Years ago as a young church planter I decided to take a ministry team to Central America. We employed the services of a minister who had set up many events for ministries in various nations. This leader was known as an expert on international ministry and team travel. We had a well-organized itinerary with every detail and facet planned accordingly.

I still remember the sense of exhilaration that I felt when I walked out of the plane onto the runway into the humid Central American air! The large team that was with me was so excited to see what Jesus was going to do during our time there. Our faith was set on a massive harvest and major miracles. We had a number of events set up during our trip. One of these events was an outdoor evangelistic campaign, where we were going to pray for the impossible, ask God for miracles, and then cast the net of salvation. The organizer of this trip had set up similar campaigns in nations all over the globe with great success. We were stepping foot into a nation where none of us had ever been, including our organizer.

We arrived the first night at the outdoor event and were surprised at what appeared to be a disappointing response! Our event organizer followed the same pattern of promotion and structure that was used with much success in other nations, yet the attendance was sparse. You could feel a blanket of discouragement come over our team. To top it off, we had been encountering severe demonic warfare during this trip on multiple fronts! People had been physically attacked, others had severe spiritual attacks, and the entire team had experienced a heightened state of resistance.

What should I do? This was the question that was racing through my mind at the campaign. I knew deep in my heart that it was the purpose and plan of the Lord for us to be in that nation, yet how could this campaign turn out like this? We had spent a large amount of money on organization and promotion. We had prayed and sought the Lord for this trip. We had a very high expectation of attendance and of what God was going to do. It felt like we were deflated balloons! In spite of it all, we were with a small group that had gathered there, so we had to press on.

As I prayed, I could feel such a battle for the destiny of the team and the outcome of the trip! The whole thing was hanging in the balance. I did the one thing that I knew to do in the midst of attack; I sought the Lord. Suddenly He revealed to me that there was someone in the meeting who was deaf and mute. He told me that one miracle would break the whole thing wide open. I told the team what I had heard, and we began to look for the person whom the Lord was spotlighting. We found the man. With a boldness that only comes from heaven, I told the crowd that I knew Jesus would heal him as we prayed. What a step of faith! If this did not happen, the whole trip could be ruined. There is a realm of faith when you just know in your spirit what the Lord has said, and you are not moved by anything else. I was functioning in the gift of faith in that moment. We prayed for the man, and God healed him in front of everyone! The first word that he spoke was Jesus! With that miracle the clouds of gloom pushed back, and we broke through. People were saved, healed, and set free that night.

We have continued working in that region of the nation with many wonderful stories of God's power. The enemy was doing all that he could to abort the assignment before it ever got going. He wanted to shut down kingdom plans. Thank

God we pressed through! There have been ups and downs in our ministry to that region in the years since, but that night was a turning point. We were either breaking through or surrendering, and we chose to push on.

THE FRUIT OF OBEDIENCE

There truly is a grace, authority, anointing, and blessing on obedience. The Bible tells us that if we are both willing and obedient, we will eat the good of the land (Isa. 1:19). We must be willing, cooperative, have a right heart, and follow the Holy Spirit to enter the will of God. We must also be obedient and fully committed to doing His will. When we fulfill all these requirements, we have something powerful.

But if we lack any of them, we won't be fully equipped to walk through seasons in which we must radically move with God in an act of obedience that makes no sense to our natural understanding. It is in those seasons that our spiritual senses must be alert in order to override our natural minds and enable us to embark on the journey of faith and dedication.

Very often an exploit of God begins with a radical commission. Let me say it this way: you will rarely experience a major miracle without first being willing to take a tremendous risk. This is why a dedicated relationship with the Holy Spirit is so critical. You must be tuned in to His voice, perceptive and ready to act when He speaks. When you embark on the pathway of obedience, it is of utmost importance that you learn to establish your heart in peace so that your feet will not be moved in adverse times.

There is a geographical place of destiny; God has a *rechoboth* place for each of us. The word *rechoboth* means "broad places," or places of abundance and blessing![6] It is a place of harvest and reward. I believe that God has that *rechoboth* place for each one of us as we obey Him. He has created times, seasons, and places of fulfillment for your life. He alone holds the key to each dream He has given you. He will reveal the key and then invite you to take it to unlock the next door of purpose in your life.

Moving in sync with divine plans is a breathtaking adventure. When you trust God with your life, plans, and steps, it is awesome to see what He does. There are divine plans for you. Where you are matters. Who you are with matters. Seasons matter. Steps of obedience matter. When you sync up with heaven, you are led to be in the right place at the right time with the right people enjoying the right plans! There is nothing better. It is peace that will lead us and peace that will hold us.

Chapter Seven

ATTACK SYMPTOM 5—
UNUSUALLY SLUGGISH AND TIRED

▼▼▼▼▼▼▼▼▼▼▼▼▼

U NDER THE EXTREME pressure of a spiritual attack a
person finds himself unusually sluggish and tired.
Many times when I speak about this symptom of an attack
the following question arises: Couldn't that just be a natural occurrence or health condition? The answer is yes, it
could be. If a person isn't getting proper rest or is pushing
his body to the limit, then obviously he will be tired. As I
stated previously, the list of symptoms in this book provides
a checklist for a person who is attempting to discern if he is
under attack.

I have seen many people delivered from the power of a
demonic onslaught. Often they have shared with me physical
and emotional symptoms they have had. I vividly remember
a time many years ago, when I was leading a Bible college,
that a student received prayer during the morning prayer
time. The Lord revealed to the prayer team and me that she
was under the influence of a wrong spirit. As we began to
pray and intercede, the enemy began to manifest. We prayed
strongly with authority until we broke the power of hell from
her. Afterward she felt that she needed to go home for the
day. When we asked why, she said she was very sick in her
stomach. Why was she feeling that way? It was her body's
reaction to the tormenting spirit tearing and manifesting as
we broke its power. We advised her to sit for a while until she

felt better. She quickly recovered, went back to class, stayed free, and eventually graduated with honors.

During an extended attack there is typically an increase in emotional battles. As we have established in previous chapters, this is part of the coordinated efforts of the enemy. He desires to assault on multiple fronts in order to bring forth his agenda of defeat and aborted assignments. As the mind and emotions process the stress, it takes a toll on the body and on energy levels. This is illustrated when Jesus delivered a child who was held in a demonic grip. The boy's father had literally exhausted himself with futile attempts to help his son:

> One in the crowd answered, "Teacher, I brought You my son, who has a mute spirit. Wherever it takes hold on him, it dashes him to the ground. And he foams at the mouth and gnashes with his teeth and becomes rigid. And I told Your disciples so that they would cast it out, but they could not."
>
> He answered, "O faithless generation, how long shall I be with you? How long shall I bear with you? Bring him to Me."
>
> So they brought the boy to Him. When he saw Him, immediately the spirit dashed him, and he fell on the ground and wallowed, foaming at the mouth.
>
> He asked his father, "How long has it been since it came to him?"
>
> He said, "From childhood. Often it has thrown him into the fire and into the water to kill him. But if You can do anything, have compassion on us and help us."
>
> Jesus said, "If you can believe, all things are possible to him who believes."
>
> Immediately the father of the child cried out with tears, "Lord, I believe. Help my unbelief!"
>
> When Jesus saw that the people came running together, He rebuked the foul spirit, saying to it, "You

mute and deaf spirit, I command you, come out of him,
and enter him no more."

The spirit cried out and convulsed him greatly. But
it came out of him, and he was as dead, so that many
said, "He is dead." But Jesus took him by the hand and
lifted him up, and he arose.

—MARK 9:17–27

This desperate father had brought his son to the disciples, but they could not free him. Jesus rebuked them and
taught that faith is key to deliverance. In order to displace
demonic powers, we must walk in faith and be aligned with
the Word of God. Doubt creates room for the enemy. Notice
how this spirit operated. It threw this poor boy into both
water and fire in an attempt to wound or kill him. When it
was confronted by the faith and authority of Jesus, it would
knock the boy to the ground, and the child would foam at
the mouth. This shows us there is a strong physical reaction
to what is happening in the realm of the Spirit. When Jesus
cast the evil spirit out of the child, the boy convulsed and
was entirely incapacitated, like one who was dead.

There are several layers to this story. Evil spirits love to
manifest and put on a show. When a person who is afflicted
with a tormenting spirit gets around someone walking in
authority and anointing, the spirit will typically manifest
and attempt to create distraction. When a demonic force is
at work, it can and will cause physical effects, just as this boy
experienced.

EVIL SPIRITS ATTACK FROM THE OUTSIDE

The boy had a demon living in him, but a believer who is
serving the Lord and finds himself under siege is typically
being bombarded on an external level. In other words, the

foul spirit is on the outside, accusing, manifesting, twisting, and harassing.

This is what happened to Elijah when Jezebel threatened his life. He was attacked by a demonic force:

> And Ahab told Jezebel all that Elijah had done and how he had executed all the prophets with the sword. Then Jezebel sent a messenger to Elijah, saying, "So let the gods do to me and more also, if I do not make your life as the life of one of them by tomorrow about this time." When he saw that she was serious, he arose and ran for his life to Beersheba, which belongs to Judah, and left his servant there. But he went a day's journey into the wilderness and came and sat down under a juniper tree and asked that he might die, saying, "It is enough! Now, O LORD, take my life, for I am not better than my fathers." As he lay and slept under the juniper tree, an angel touched him and said to him, "Arise and eat."
> —1 KINGS 19:1–5

Elijah had just enjoyed a paramount moment of ministry. He had faced off with the evil forces in Israel and demonstrated the mighty power of God in an unprecedented fashion; he took on an army of false prophets and demonic powers and witnessed their utter defeat. God answered his call for spiritual clarity in front of the entire nation, proving His divinity and authority. The extreme battle in the spirit seemed to be over: God's fire fell and consumed the sacrifice Elijah presented. The power of Yahweh was manifested to a generation of Israelites who doubted Him.

It would seem that on the heels of such a tremendous victory the prophet would go forth with great confidence and assurance. The most significant moment of the high call of ministry in his life had just occurred. No limits had been placed on what God could do through him and for the people of Israel. The greatest days of the prophetic ministry and Elijah's role in it should have been just around the corner.

Yet despite all the promise and potential that victory created, there was a diabolical plan unfolding. Behind the scenes the nasty Jezebel spirit was planning its revenge and scheming to release a massive wave of intimidation, fear, and defeat against God's victorious prophet.

This is often the case in our lives and destinies too. We press in, pray, and prophesy, believing for life-changing breakthrough. When the victory comes, we breathe a sigh of relief, feeling as though the storm has passed and we now can relax. At such a time we absolutely should enjoy the blessings and authority of our Father, yet we must also maintain a prophetic lens that is focused on the spiritual climate and receiving warnings of counterattacks.

WORD CURSES AND WICKED PROCLAMATIONS

Instead of standing on the mountaintop of prophetic victory, Elijah was about to navigate the lonely valley of spiritual attack. The Jezebel spirit sent a messenger to Elijah to release a demonic word curse against him.

What is a word curse? First let's examine the actual meaning of *curse*. It is defined as "a solemn utterance intended to invoke a supernatural power to inflict harm or punishment on someone or something."[1]

A word curse is the release of a demonic proclamation intended to establish negative and evil forces. Words are keys that open doors to the spirit realm. Everything in the spirit realm is created by words. The enemy uses evil words and utterances to tear down, bind, and afflict. Word curses reveal spiritual intentions and have evil forces attached to them.

The power of controlling spirits, spirits of confusion, spirits of intimidation, and other evil forces are released by words. You can tell when you have been the victim of a word curse by the atmosphere it releases. Atmospheres are powerful and have lasting consequences. There are many examples in the Bible of the effect of an atmosphere. One of the most telling incidents is that in which Jesus's ministry was stifled by an atmosphere of intense unbelief:

> He went away from there and came into His own country. And His disciples followed Him. When the Sabbath came, He began to teach in the synagogue. And many hearing Him were astonished, saying, "Where did this Man get this? What is this wisdom that is given Him, that even miracles are done by His hands? Is this not the carpenter, the Son of Mary and the brother of James and Joseph and Judas and Simon? Are not His sisters here with us?" And they took offense at Him. Jesus said to them, "A prophet is not without honor, except in his own country, and among his own relatives, and in his own house." He could not do any miracles there, except that He laid His hands on a few sick people and healed them. And He was amazed because of their unbelief.
>
> —MARK 6:1–6

Jesus had carried the same authority, revelation, and power everywhere else He had gone. In the other places tremendous miracles and life-giving breakthroughs had occurred. But in His own hometown there was an unseen limitation that prohibited the flow of the Spirit. What made the difference? Had Jesus let up on His prayer life? Was He preaching another gospel? Had He significantly changed the way He ministered to people? The answer to all these questions is an emphatic *no*! Jesus was carrying the exact same message and power in His own country that He had taken to other people in other places. The major difference was the atmosphere He now encountered. He was limited in what He was able to do because of the strong blanket of unbelief and offense. The atmosphere produced the different result. This example shows us the power of an atmosphere.

I had an encounter a number of years ago that reinforced these principles to me when I was ministering in El Salvador. We had been traveling all over the nation and were seeing phenomenal miracles, power, and authority in the Spirit. I don't think we had held a single meeting that had not produced some type of notable miracle.

It was the last day of our trip, and my mind and body were tired. I and the others with me had endured a grueling schedule that week, but the results were worth it all. We had traveled far away from any major city way up into the mountains to minister at a very small rural church. God began to speak to me with several words of knowledge. I was ministering in much the same way I had the entire week, yet something was lacking. As I laid hands on the people, the prayers seemed like empty words and produced no major instant results. There were a few minor healings, and people were encouraged, but there was a lack of the kind of authority and great power that we had seen manifested all week.

After the service ended, I wrestled with what had taken place. What was so different about this little church that our ministry time seemed limited in the realm of power and miracles? Why wasn't there the same flow we had seen everywhere else in that country?

My host explained that I had broken several religious traditions in the church by the way I had ministered and what I had shared. I learned that the church had deep roots in old traditions and was steeped in unbelief. I realized something that day: the atmosphere was the issue. I had ministered in the same way but with vastly different results because we were operating under a lid of unbelief and religious bondage.

We left the mountains to travel to our final gathering, and when I spoke that night, there was a vibrant flow of the miracles and power of God just as there had been at every other meeting that week. We were out of the atmosphere of unbelief and back in one where people were open to hear and receive the gospel. The soil certainly affects the seed.

Satan loves to create hard atmospheres of unbelief, confusion, and bondage in the lives of God's people. So many believers are fighting to get a breakthrough that already belongs to them. But it doesn't come because they are deceived and live in a toxic atmosphere. As an example of how an atmosphere makes a difference, think of how many times you have heard of an artist or writer traveling to a scenic destination to work. He believes the atmosphere of beauty and tranquility will help to unlock the creative gift inside of him. When he gets into that type of atmosphere, there is a free flow of ideas and artistic ability.

When someone speaks out a wicked proclamation, there is an immediate reaction of heaviness. It's a struggle to feel normal for long afterward. This is a major sign of a word curse. The evil words spoken are like a key in the spirit realm that unlocks a doorway to another dimension, creating a dark atmosphere. This is the intention of the adversary: to invoke a hindering spiritual influence.

COUNTERING WITH GOD'S WORDS

God releases creative power by words. He creates by speaking! In Romans 4:17 (AMPC), the Bible says:

> As it is written, I have made you the father of many
> nations. [He was appointed our father] in the sight of
> God in Whom he believed, Who gives life to the dead
> and speaks of the nonexistent things that [He has fore-
> told and promised] as if they [already] existed.

Likewise, we are called to function and flow in the spirit of dominion by speaking forth things from the realm of the Spirit. Words can be authoritative spiritual seeds that contain either the power of death or life. They are like containers that hold spiritual substance and influence:

> A fool's lips enter into contention, and his mouth calls
> for flogging. A fool's mouth is his destruction, and his
> lips are the snare of his soul. The words of a talebearer
> are as wounds, and they go down into the innermost
> parts of the body.
> —Proverbs 18:6–8

These verses demonstrate the utmost importance of our proclamation. There are many adults today who are still battling thoughts and influences related to word curses released over them as children. Contrary to popular opinion, words are important and are to be chosen wisely. The more a person renews his mind, the more his mouth will begin to change. We are called to hold the office of a priest, making decrees and invoking the power of the kingdom of heaven.

Satan establishes the working of demonic powers by words. He has someone give voice to his intentions in order to create a polluted atmosphere that is alive with wicked schemes. When a word curse is proclaimed, it invites ugly spirits of darkness on the scene. That is the part of the attack many people miss; as a result they do not properly discern and take authority over the power of the word curses that have been released. Regarding our authority over the works of hell, we must recognize that we can pull down the proclamation of hell and release the exact opposite outcome over our lives. We use our positional authority to govern our lives as children of God. We choose not to align with Satan's confession over us but to embrace the declaration of heaven. We release a blessing in place of the curse.

Speak the Word of God over your life and use it as a key that opens the doorway to heaven's plans and atmosphere. Take the prophetic words you have received and stand on them! Open the doorway to heaven's promises with the key words you have been given. Prophets and prophetic people release spiritual utterances to build, create, and establish, as well as to tear down by proclamation what the enemy has built. The prophetic spirit is a creative spirit that sees into another dimension and then declares what it sees. The anointing of the prophet is in the prophet's mouth. Each believer carries a dimension of the prophetic spirit on his life; you can open spiritual doors and slam other ones shut.

HOW JEZEBEL'S WORD
CURSE AFFECTED ELIJAH

When Ahab told Jezebel that Elijah had executed the prophets of Baal, he was partnering with his wife's dark desires to end true prophetic ministry in that generation. The information he provided caused her to release a powerful word curse that sent Elijah into a deep downward spiral. The prophet was almost immediately overtaken with a heavy depression that sidelined him and knocked the spiritual wind out of him. Knowing that this came right after his great victory lets us know the enemy is ruthless and loves to counterattack.

After he heard Jezebel's message, Elijah fell into an unusually deep sleep. This was not a peaceful rest resulting from his spiritual exertion against the false prophets. Rather, he had become both physically and emotionally exhausted because the atmosphere around him was heavy with defeat. He had succumbed to the spiritual attack that had been launched against him.

Jezebel had assigned a messenger to deliver the evil utterance. That is a tactic of a spiritual attack—using messengers to speak out the lying accusations of the enemy and release word curses. Elijah lay in a state of uninterrupted slumber. He could not be awakened, so God sent an angel to him. Under the immense burden of demonic power, his mind and body shut down. He retreated into a position of docile surrender. The siege of the Jezebel spirit had taken an immense toll on him.

I absolutely despise the evil Jezebel spirit. It hates the prophetic, seduces people, and plots the destruction of entire generations. The Jezebel spirit makes war against God's leaders, attempting to abort and overthrow the destiny the Lord has planned for them.

DELILAH AND THE CONSPIRACY OF EVIL

In the same way that a messenger of evil was dispatched against Elijah, Delilah was sent by the enemy into the life of the great champion Samson. She was on assignment, and her job was to steal his strength and stop his progress.

Samson was a fierce weapon in the Lord's hand, endued with strength that no other person possessed. He single-handedly wiped out scores of God's adversaries. His anointing manifested through uncommon strength, and he was a tremendous threat to the kingdom of the enemy. As amazing as his strength was, Samson also had an abiding weakness: his lust for women. The enemy knew exactly which part of his emotions and humanity to attack.

We must grasp this important point about the powers of darkness: Satan studies us to know when and where to strike. He lured Samson off course and into disobedience through a relationship with a beautiful woman. Samson was a Nazirite; for that reason alone he never should have started any type of liaison with Delilah.

His relationship with her grew beyond physical lust to become an emotional attachment. It blinded him, or he would have perceived that secretly amid their growing affair she was plotting with the Philistines against him:

> After this Samson loved a woman in the Valley of Sorek, whose name was Delilah. The Philistine rulers came up to her and said, "Trick him! Find out about how his strength is so great and how we can overcome him, bind him, and humiliate him. Each one of us will give you eleven hundred silver coins."
>
> —JUDGES 16:4–5

The villainous scheme hatched between Delilah and the Philistines exposes a spiritual reality: evil spirits typically work together. They are like a pack of ravaging wolves roaming the landscape in search of prey. Jesus taught that one unclean spirit partners with others to create havoc and unfold the works of darkness in a person's life:

> When an unclean spirit goes out of a man, it passes through dry places seeking rest, but finds none. Then it says, "I will return to my house from which I came." And when it comes, it finds it empty, swept, and put in order. Then it goes and brings with itself seven other spirits more evil than itself, and they enter and dwell there. And the last state of that man is worse than the first. So shall it be also with this evil generation.
>
> —MATTHEW 12:43–45

Jesus explains a sad reality many people do not realize: when they yield to the influence of a particular bondage, a wider web than the one they can see is always being spun for them. The plans of hell are to bind and ensnare a person on *many* levels.

When a particular plot is released against a person, layers of heinous operations are added. Delilah was the initial temptation that came to Samson, but there were other partners in evil awaiting him. So many times people do not realize these tactics. They see only what is right in front of them, not realizing other spirits are involved, attempting to bind them and rob the life-giving anointing from their life.

What was Samson doing while Delilah was deceiving him? The Bible says she had lulled him to sleep on her lap! She continually turned him over for destruction, yet he was blinded to the reality of what was happening. She had deceived him. Deception is always foundational to the devil's operations. He brings in deception to twist the mind so the person involved does not discern what is happening and cannot get free from his sticky web.

As his life was gradually being stolen and his purpose being thwarted, Samson was asleep, both physically and spiritually. The strong warrior had no energy to fight off the impending doom. His mind and body were in a state of unusual exhaustion.

THE POWER OF THE HOLY SPIRIT IS THE ANSWER

Samson was unaware of what was going on right beneath his nose! Elijah was struck down at the height of his ministry and under the influence of a deep sleep while hiding in a cave. Each of these men was under a spiritual attack that drained his natural energy and put his mind in a lull.

Have you found yourself struggling to take on all the responsibilities of life? Has it been difficult to find your "get up and go"? A lack of energy is one of the wearying side effects of the enemy's prolonged bombardment. Uncommon weariness is dispatched to rob vitality and spiritual discernment.

A mind and body that has been in intense battle becomes drained. That's why unusual and prolonged exhaustion can be the fruit of a spiritual attack and may indicate the need to break the siege to release the life of God. There is a vibrancy in the Spirit that is available for every believer; we do not have to succumb to the desires of the wicked one or remain in the cave of fatigue. The life-giving power of the Holy Spirit can bring us out from under this symptom, enabling us to go forth with renewed energy and focus.

Chapter Eight

ATTACK SYMPTOM 6—
STRONG URGE TO
QUIT ASSIGNMENT

▼▼▼▼▼▼▼▼▼▼▼▼▼

O NE OF THE marks of an evil attack is the strong urge to quit the assignment God has given you. The enemy releases warfare against the mind of a believer with continual corrupt indictments. The target is your destiny. The dark weapons are employed in a demonic strategy to remove a person from his assigned place.

Rebecca Greenwood, cofounder and president of Christian Harvest International, explains the power of mental warfare in her article "7 Ways to Disarm Strongholds of the Mind," published by *Charisma* magazine. "Our thought lives are the pioneers that lead to what will play out in our lives personally, emotionally, spiritually, and will even influence how we step into God's plan for our lives," she writes. "However, circumstances have the opportunity to greatly affect what we believe about ourselves. Not to mention, we have an enemy who will take advantage of negative circumstances to speak lies, which become strongholds."[1]

As I have established already in this book, the enemy coordinates circumstances during a period of attack that are aimed at bringing discouragement and defeat. Negative experiences lead to the building up of emotional walls, thought patterns, and long-term strongholds of the mind (systems of thought). The mind goes into defense mode to protect from ongoing pain. The emotional walls are established and for-tified to keep people from penetrating further and creating more hurt. The problem with this defensive buildup is that it also prevents healthy relationships from being established. A traumatized mind can easily become a toxic place of ongoing pain, unhealthy mental patterns, and unresolved conflict. The healing power of Jesus is imperative in the life of a person who has gone through emotional stress and trauma.

Greenwood further explains this process: "One of Satan's tactics is mental warfare. Over time, he causes a battle to rage in our mind that keeps us feeling accused and intimidated. It is no mistake that he is called the 'accuser of the brethren' (see Rev. 12:10). He uses false guilt and tormenting thoughts to remind us of our past failures, or he speaks lies against us trying to cripple our Christian walk. He will invade our thought life, causing us to embrace wrong thinking, bad atti-tudes and emotional scars."[2]

DON'T ABANDON COURSE

Amid the onslaught of intense emotional and spiritual pressure it is easy to make a foolish decision. The enemy is standing right there prompting you to quit, whispering his lies to paint a false picture of peace for you, if only you will abandon your post. This is one of his primary goals in tempting and attacking us. His tactic is to get us to forfeit our appointed place of destiny, grace, and provision. He wants to spoil our inheritance and cause us to vacate what rightfully belongs to us. He uses immense tension, lies, and ongoing strain to convince us to move.

These are the moments when we must dig in, plant our feet, and refuse to budge! It is in these times of fiery testing that we have to be fully convinced that what God said is ours—and refuse to budge! There can be no middle ground.

We must be established in God's will for our lives, and we must be doing our best to travel the road He has laid out for us. There is not only divine guidance but also wonderful grace for the journey.

The sad reality is that at this very moment there are men and women living with an overwhelming sense of regret because they gave in to an attack. In the middle of the fight, when the pressure seemed too great, they abandoned course. They laid down the call and walked away from their destiny. They chose the pathway of comfort and normality instead of striving to live out their appointed purpose.

In the midst of the conflict you must avoid making a rash decision. It is very easy to take a wrong turn when you make a move in reaction to the crushing weight of the enemy's ploys. Wisdom weighs it out: it does not move too fast, and it seeks wise counsel. This is a major key to avoiding the enemy's devices. Take time to seek out those who have another perspective and can see what you do not see. If you are surrounded by crisis, you are not seeing with panoramic vision. You are focused on what is in your immediate line of sight. You need to hear from people who are posted on a higher plane above the crisis.

The Lord holds the answer to every question that we may struggle with in the battle, and He makes His wisdom available to us:

> The proverbs of Solomon, the son of David, king of Israel: To know wisdom and instruction, to perceive the words of understanding, to receive the instruction of wisdom, justice, judgment, and equity; to give subtlety to the simple, to the young man knowledge and discretion—a wise man will hear and will increase learning, and a man of understanding will attain wise counsel, to understand a proverb and the interpretation,

the words of the wise and their riddles. The fear of the
LORD is the beginning of knowledge, but fools despise
wisdom and instruction.

—PROVERBS 1:1–7

Therefore we must not surrender to the screaming voice
of our flesh or do something that we will regret later. We
must build our lives on enduring principles of godly character, biblical insight, and Spirit leading.

WALKING IN THE SPIRIT

The eighth chapter of Romans reveals the walk of the Spirit—
which is so critical for us to follow. In it the Apostle Paul
paints a vivid picture of our spiritual journey by comparing
it to walking a pathway or road. God has provided and illu-
minated a pathway of spiritual progression that we are to
walk on. He has established a road map for us by which we
can move deeper into the things of the Spirit. We are called
to proceed down the pathway of destiny one step at a time.
We move from one place in the Spirit to another as we tap
into divine revelation, illumination, and understanding.

The Holy Spirit is our great teacher! Jesus said in John
14:25–26, "I have spoken these things to you while I am still
with you. But the Counselor, the Holy Spirit, whom the
Father will send in My name, will teach you everything and
remind you of all that I told you."

The precious Holy Spirit was sent to empower, endue,
renew, cleanse, lead, guide, and teach us. When we become
acquainted with the person of the Holy Spirit, we tap into
another dimension of our spiritual life. Continual fellowship
with God opens up the walk of the Spirit to us. We are no
longer led by our feelings but by the abiding peace of God.

This powerful peace easily secures our minds and emotions in times of crisis.

Far too many believers are judging assignments that carry eternal rewards in the light of momentary circumstances. The Bible calls us to do the opposite: to judge momentary circumstances in the light of their eternal purpose:

> Our light affliction, which lasts but for a moment, works for us a far more exceeding and eternal weight of glory, while we do not look at the things which are seen, but at the things which are not seen. For the things which are seen are temporal, but the things which are not seen are eternal.
> —2 Corinthians 4:17–18

We are specifically commissioned to live with our eyes focused on eternity! The enemy can twist and attack the natural things around us, he can attempt to overwhelm or bombard our minds, but he cannot abort the will of God. One of his devious tricks is getting us to focus more on the temporary condition of our lives than on the enduring call of God. Ratcheting up the accusations, condemning whispers, and heavy burdens, he attempts to get us to change our minds. He wants us to throw up our hands and surrender.

He will use all kinds of tricky reasoning. He will even twist scriptures and use silly religious sayings in his evil attempts to convince us to abort destiny. This is why 2 Corinthians 4:17–18 is so clear, because we are not called to live our lives based on the natural realm but on the spirit realm.

The walk of the Spirit is often very disconnected from our natural circumstances; the two can seem out of sync with each other. But we are to move forward based on the *rhema* (spoken word) of God, not on our circumstances. Many Christians judge the will of God in their lives by the

temporary circumstances that they are facing. They fail to
see the bigger picture that He sees. Taking a step of faith
and obeying an instruction, however, launches us into the
unknown. Walking by faith moves us far beyond our comfort zone.

You cannot make a rash decision when adversity arises or
second-guess the leading of the Holy Spirit because there is
conflict. A believer who moves each time an attack comes
does not have a strong spiritual root system. He is not rooted
deeply in faith, or in the Word of God. His prayer life is
shallow, and he is easily swayed. Jesus did not call us to be
good starters; He calls us to finish the race! Far too many
people are really great at beginning something, but they
always make excuses for quitting when things get tough. We
desperately need some strong finishers in the body of Christ.
We need people with deep roots who will stand during the
storm and remain convinced that what God promised is a
reality, no matter what the circumstances look like in the
moment.

IT'S NOT ALL SMOOTH SAILING

A false narrative is being given to the current generation
of believers, creating the illusion that they will never face
any bumps in the road to the kingdom. Many have taught
that when you obey God, you will enjoy smooth sailing in
everything. Yes, we serve a God who has authority over the
winds and the waves, a God who has given us full access to
kingdom power so that we can speak to storms and command them to be still, as He did. And yes, we can absolutely
enjoy a life that is cemented in His perfect will and filled
with uncommon peace.

But it's also true that sometimes storms arise in the center
of a kingdom assignment. Many of our heroes in the faith

who stepped out in faith on a word from the Lord, pioneering a bold path of the miraculous and forging ahead in radical faith and obedience, encountered storms. In fact, we probably would never have known their names if it were not for the winds of adversity they overcame. Their stories were told because of how they responded when the storm rose against them. The real truth is that champions are born in the midst of opposition. They rise above the lies, the pain, and the struggle—and they slay the enemy.

Mark 4:35–40 describes a time when Jesus sent His disciples on a journey. He gave them clear instructions about where to go and how to get there. Notice it was while they were in the boat, in the center of the will of God, that a storm arose! They were not in disobedience—not at all. They were, in fact, doing what they had been commanded to do when the storm hit:

> That same day, when the evening came, He said to them, "Let us go cross to the other side." When they had sent the crowd away, they took Him in the boat just as He was. There were also other little boats with Him. A great windstorm arose, and the waves splashed into the boat, so that it was now filling the boat. He was in the stern asleep on a pillow. They woke Him and said, "Teacher, do You not care that we are perishing?" He rose and rebuked the wind, and said to the sea, "Peace, be still!" Then the wind ceased and there was a great calm. He said to them, "Why are you so fearful? How is that you have no faith?"
>
> —MARK 4:35–40

Jesus's word of instruction was precise: "Let us go cross to the other side"! God had declared His will to the disciples. There was no second word, just the one primary instruction.

Yet in the process of obeying, the disciples encountered a fierce storm that had come to shake their resolve. They should have been steadfast, resting in what God had already declared, but they were not. They gave in to fear and questioned what He had said.

Notice that Jesus rebuked their lack of faith. In His heart and mind, when He had spoken the instruction, it was settled. There was enough power in the word of the Lord to bring them out on the other side. This is a picture of what happens in our own lives. The Lord speaks to us, we step forward in obedience, but then the enemy sends adversity. He tosses us back and forth with natural and emotional turbulence. His goal is to get us to give in to fear, question what the Lord has said, and ultimately give up.

HOW TO RESPOND TO THE STORMS

By contrast, how did Jesus respond to the storm? He commanded it! How are we to deal with storms? We are to rise up in authority and command the elements. When intense wavering is trying to overtake our human understanding, we are to command our minds. When the voice of Satan is raging, we are to command him to be silent. When the waves of fear are battering our obedience, we are to decree the spirit of love, power, and a sound mind according to 2 Timothy 1:7 (NKJV).

Faith doesn't ask, plead, or beg; it stands, decrees, commands, and receives. Emotional and spiritual instability, however, cause you to waver on what God has already declared:

> If any of you lacks wisdom, let him ask of God, who gives to all men liberally and without criticism, and it will be given to him. But let him ask in faith, without wavering. For he who wavers is like a wave of the sea,

driven and tossed with the wind. Let not that man think that he will receive anything from the Lord. A double-minded man is unstable in all his ways.

—JAMES 1:5–8

A declaration of heaven is a done deal in the mind of the Lord. There is great creative ability in the word spoken by the Lord. When He speaks, an unlocking occurs in our lives and in the realm of the spirit. Our job is to align our hearts and minds with what God has already declared.

The words of the Lord are infused with strength and life. One of the secrets to spiritual longevity and success is to meditate on what God has declared over our lives and boldly stand on it as though it were accomplished, for in the spirit realm it is already finished. The moment God declared it, it was done on our behalf. As we think on both His written Word and also His spoken word to us, there is a release of supernatural peace, strength, and faith.

An unstable man does not receive the promise (James 1:7). Faith is the result of the spoken word of God (Rom. 10:17). When God speaks to us, our hearts are established in faith. Faith does not back down just because there is a change in circumstances. On the contrary, faith digs in its heels and puts a demand on the promise to move and change the circumstances.

A man or woman who develops a strong walk in the Spirit does not survey the natural landscape before stepping out. After they have heard from God, they advance with great tenacity, convinced of the will of God. They move forward and refuse to look back.

You cannot allow your mind to camp out with all the negative what-ifs: What if this doesn't work? What if my friends think I am crazy? What if I fail? What if I don't have the resources? The fact is that a bold step of faith will not ask the what-if questions; it will always require you to move far beyond your natural talents, resources, and abilities and rely on Jesus like never before. It is part of the adventure.

STAND FAST IN FAITH

So many people tell me they are unsure about what Jesus has told them to do because they do not feel qualified. Many times they say they don't even know how to do what the Lord is asking them to do. I laugh because this has been my life story! Time after time the Lord has asked me to step out and walk in the unknown. He challenges my level of reliance on Him. When He places me in a position that I am not qualified for or don't have the talent to fulfill, then I have only one option, and that is to be entirely dependent on Him.

That is exactly where He wants you and me—in that place where we tap inner strength and release the miraculous realm in our own lives and the lives of others. He asks us over and over again to plunge into the deep side of the pool of faith. He leads us out until the water is over our heads.

I remember an episode in my own life a number of years ago that taught me a valuable lesson about the walk of the Spirit and radical obedience. My beautiful wife and I had just made a major ministry transition. We were really enjoying the new season in which we were living. I was traveling a lot and conducting powerful meetings. We had traveled to Virginia, and revival broke out where I was preaching. God was doing powerful miracles, people were being saved, and God's power was going forth in a very strong way. During that time the Lord spoke very clearly to me about moving to Virginia. It was the last thing on my mind. My wife and I were living in Tennessee at the time and were very happy there.

We prayed, and over a period of time we became convinced

that it was the will of God for us to move. We began to make arrangements, but there was heavy resistance. It seemed as if none of the natural things were lining up, even though we had been given divine direction. If I had been like some believers, I would have just assumed that the resistance meant God had changed His mind or I had not heard Him correctly. Thank God I knew better than to think like that. I knew that after God speaks, we are not to let go of what He said, no matter what goes on.

Several of my Christian friends became like Job's comforters, planting seeds of discouragement and unbelief. They told me that if it was truly God's will, then everything would fall in place.

Now, let me expound here. I absolutely believe in the goodness and provision of the Father. I believe that He goes ahead of us, securing all that is needed to accomplish His good plans for us. That said, I also believe there are times when the camp of the enemy opposes the will of God. In those times he is trying to create a high level of frustration and use it to urge us to give up. To counter that, we must stand strong on the word of the Lord to us and continue moving toward the will of God.

The day before we were to move, all of our housing plans fell through. Again, it seemed as though nothing was working out. But we had a word from God. People asked me what I was going to do. I responded, "I am going to load the truck and move!" We packed up and headed out; we were on a great faith adventure. We did not have everything lined up, in the natural. But we had a bold instruction from God, and we were not shaken by the attacks. When we arrived in Virginia, the Lord had already gone ahead of us and prepared the way. We had provision on every front and began a powerful new season of ministry.

Follow the Leading of the Spirit

In the midst of that transition there were multiple opportunities to give up. That is the enemy's trick! The reason he applies so much pressure and comes so hard against the will of God is to get people to relinquish their proper place. He creates mounting tension and uncomfortable situations to thwart the direction the Holy Spirit has placed in our hearts. The goal is to move us away from the will of God.

This is why it is imperative that we recognize the leading of the Holy Spirit and move in unison with His voice, not our present circumstances. The walk of the Spirit positions us in a place where internal leading and knowing are sometimes completely disconnected from outward circumstances.

During an attack the enemy fights against our position in the kingdom, geographical destiny, divine relationships, and kingdom gifting. Demonic powers gleefully hurl lies at our minds in an ongoing effort to convince us to quit. The tremendous heaviness that manifests in a season of spiritual struggle creates a weighty atmosphere, causing the mind to engage in thoughts of changing courses, abandoning plans, and surrendering to the struggle.

I can remember another time when I was very young in the ministry and enduring an ongoing spiritual attack. In this battle there were multiple layers at play. A typical attack will come with shaking on several fronts simultaneously. That was the case in my life at the time.

The pressure on my emotions mounted and intensified. An intense desire was arising inside me to change course. At the time I was in a ministry position, leading a group of people. The enemy began to paint a false picture of tranquility—a picture of how my life would look if I would just give up my present assignment and head in another direction. I began to embrace the false leading, believing that perhaps it was the will of God.

In truth, I was yielding to the strong urge to quit my assignment, but I wasn't properly discerning the source of the leading. One of my spiritual leaders and mentors identified this directional change as being a lie from hell. He told me I needed to break the deception and hold fast to my post in ministry. I simply could not see what he was seeing.

As this was going on, I attended a meeting at my local church. A powerful prophetic minister prayed over me. He began to speak the word of the Lord over my life and expose the weapons of the enemy. It was as though mud was suddenly wiped off the windshield of my mind. Vision was restored. The combination of wise counsel and life-giving prophetic ministry broke the deception of the enemy and reignited the fire inside me.

I thank God for the strong, bold voices He has placed in my life through the years. Many people are taken out of their destiny because either they do not have wise counsel, or they refuse to listen to it. Having been in ministry since I was very young, I have had the unfortunate experience of seeing many people who were called and appointed become sidelined by the work of the enemy. For the majority of them there were people in their lives warning them and declaring the will of the Lord to them. Prophetic warnings and wise counsel must be heeded if shipwreck is to be avoided.

Make no mistake about it; the enemy wants to take you out. He has designed evil schemes to derail God's glorious plans for you. When you are in the heat of battle, you desperately need strong voices of truth to advise you. You also need hearing ears and a tender heart.

In the Bible prophets are called "trumpets" (Isa. 58:1; Jer. 6:17). They sound the alarm, expose the battle, and issue the call. The prophetic anointing can break through the enemy's lies and call you back to purpose. It is one of the powerful instruments of war God uses to deliver His people in the time of crisis. Prophetic people discern the attack and release the words of the Lord.

Having wise voices in your life adds a layer of spiritual wisdom and guidance that protects you from deception. It's a benefit of having a good spiritual family and healthy relationships with godly leaders. They can speak into your life both in times of blessing and discouragement, helping to keep you on course:

> Folly is joy to him who is destitute of wisdom, but a man of understanding walks uprightly. Without counsel, purposes are disappointed, but in the multitude of counselors they are established.
> —PROVERBS 15:21–22

The bottom line is this: You must hold fast to what God has said about your life. You must develop deep roots of faith and prophetic insight. You must not make a snap decision in the midst of struggle. Weighty pressure from the enemy comes to push you out of your assigned place, but you can endure and overcome!

Chapter Nine

ATTACK SYMPTOM 7—
DRAWN BACK TOWARD
OLD BONDAGES

▼▼▼▼▼▼▼▼▼▼▼▼

WHEN THE LORD sets you free, He doesn't provide just partial freedom. He doesn't make you free for a season and then place bondage back on you. He didn't win an incomplete victory over the enemy. He went to the cross with our absolute freedom, healing, victory, and salvation in mind.

Deliverance from demonic bondages was one of the hallmarks of Jesus's earthly ministry. Everywhere He traveled, He set the captives free. The Bible tells us that He is the same yesterday, today, and forever (Heb. 13:8). As you surrender your life fully to Christ, you are delivered from destructive cycles, bondages, fears, and the snare of sin. Jesus sets you totally free:

> Therefore if the Son sets you free, you shall be free indeed.
>
> —JOHN 8:36

The reality is that the enemy hates your freedom. The powers of hell are dedicated to dragging you and me through the mud. They work tirelessly to find a way into our lives in order to ensnare us again. I am not saying that we should live in fear of the enemy. On the contrary, we should walk in great confidence in the power of God and the victory that belongs to us. We should bind up devils and stand on the Word every chance we get. We should boldly and forcefully execute the plans of the kingdom.

We should also be aware of his tactics. This is where so many people miss it. They are simply unaware of the reality of the spirit realm and the diabolical plans of the enemy. They live without being in tune with what is taking place in the dimension of the spirit. I have seen people wonderfully set free from a particular thing, without realizing that the enemy would love to come back through a little crack. They may have received a prophetic warning, but they allow the enemy to make them think the caution was spoken in a negative spirit and they don't have to be concerned about it. They are unaware and out of tune, and that is a wide-open door for the power of the enemy.

In a sustained spiritual battle you may be tempted and drawn back toward negative cycles from which Jesus delivered you. The extreme pressure that mounts during an attack is an attempt to overwhelm your mind and emotions, making you vulnerable to temptation. Many times a person is set free from a particular habit or vice, but the pressure makes them stressed, weakened, and spiritually vulnerable.

There are two reasons you need to understand this particular symptom of a spiritual attack:

1. *You must identify the attack before you can break it.* These symptoms help you to recognize what is happening in the spirit realm.

2. *You must realize the goal of the attack to resist it.* The enemy would like nothing better than to drag you back into the place from which God has delivered you. He would take great joy in getting you to yield to an old habit or

partake in an old bondage. Once you have
made the mistake, he will move in with heaps
of accusation and condemnation. It is Satan's
desire to enslave you again with the very
things God delivered you from.

One of the signs of spiritual breakthrough and release is
when the Holy Spirit sets a person free from negative spiritual and emotional cycles. Every believer is invited to leave
the road of fear and destruction and embrace the victory
that has been provided for them at Calvary. Each of us has
access to a brand-new nature that looks, thinks, and talks
like God's. Your inner man does not get out of bed depressed
or fearful. Your spirit man has the very life of God pulsating
through every part. That's why, as Christians, we are called
to live differently from the world and put aside the deeds that
were inspired by our old nature:

Therefore this I say and testify in the Lord, that from
now on you walk not as other Gentiles walk, in the
vanity of their minds, having their understanding
darkened, excluded from the life of God through the
ignorance that is within them, due to the hardness of
their hearts. Being calloused they have given themselves over to sensuality for the practice of every kind of
impurity with greediness. But you did not learn about
Christ in this manner, if indeed you have heard Him
and have been taught by Him, as the truth is in Jesus:
that you put off the former way of life in the old nature,
which is corrupt according to the deceitful lusts, and
be renewed in the spirit of your mind; and that you
put on the new nature, which was created according to
God in righteousness and true holiness.

—EPHESIANS 4:17–24

How can we do what the Word says we should do in this passage? The Apostle Paul gives us the answer in Romans 7–8. In chapter 7 he chronicles the weakness of the flesh. He reveals its desire to fulfill selfish lusts and not walk in the ways of God and explains the intense warfare between the natural man and the spirit man. In Romans 8 he shows us that the answer to the lusts and weaknesses of the flesh is in walking in our new nature and living out of our spirit man and not the carnal man.

All of us have faced our own battles between our carnal nature (our flesh) and our spiritual nature. For each of us there have been moments when we allowed our natural mind to override our inner leading. There have been seasons when we knew what the Father wanted us to do, but we seemed to keep failing and walking down the pathway of the flesh. Our flesh is filled with lustful desires and selfish ambitions.

GOD'S PLANS FOR US

We are called to walk in a higher place. As new creations in Jesus we have full access to the spirit realm. We can walk with God and overcome the temptations of the enemy. We can build our inner man and develop strong spiritual muscles. We can meditate on the Word of God and sharpen our spiritual understanding. We can live transformed lives and do great exploits.

The victory takes place on the inside. As we learn to build up our spirit man and live out of our new nature, then we begin to walk and talk differently. Inward transformation brings supernatural change to outward living; a born-again man has been powerfully renewed, changed, and re-created.

The powerful work of the Spirit in our lives brings renewal. He does a life-changing work of regeneration in us. What is regeneration? It is the impartation of life instead of death, the release of grace instead of bondage, the flowing of rich wells of love, and the complete change of the spirit of man. Titus 3:4–6 describes it this way:

> But when the kindness and the love of God our Savior toward mankind appeared, not by works of righteousness which we have done, but according to His mercy He saved us, through the washing of rebirth and the renewal of the Holy Spirit, whom He poured out on us abundantly through Jesus Christ our Savior.

God has good plans for everyone when they are born. He has mighty kingdom exploits already mapped out for us. It is completely impossible to spend any amount of time in the Word of God without discovering how masterfully He created destiny for each one of His children. Not only are moments of destiny planned, but also an entire pathway is charted out and covered in grace for every person who lives now or ever has lived. This is one of the things that makes God, God. Nobody else could execute such precise plans on a grand scale like that.

THE ENEMY'S PLANS

Unfortunately the enemy also has plans—plans of defeat and destruction. I remember hearing several years ago a frightening vision that had been given to a minister. He saw a delivery room in a hospital, and evil spirits were there, plotting how to attach themselves to each child. Each foul spirit carried a different evil nature and planned to attack a child when he or she entered the world. Can you imagine this horrible picture? A spirit of lust decides to influence a person at the very beginning of his life, and he has an ongoing struggle with that particular temptation.

But I also want to be clear that I do not believe we are

called to live a single moment of our lives in fear of the enemy's plans. In fact, I am thoroughly convinced of the authority that God gave us to plunder the works of the enemy and to live free of his plans. We can pray for our families and break each assignment. The blood of Jesus, the name of Jesus, and the Word of God are much mightier than any little demonic imp trespassing on God's property (you, me, and our loved ones)!

Back to my point: Satan and his minions attempt to establish an evil pathway for a person's life at an early age. They coordinate negative events to initiate emotional bondages in order to cripple faith and paralyze progress. Many people grow up under a weight that opens the door for negative emotional cycles.

In the salvation experience there is a powerful invitation to complete freedom. Part of our journey into the new nature is breaking off the old way of thinking. We begin to dive deep into the Word of God and change our thought patterns. As we change how we think, we change how we speak. We begin to align our confession with God's Word. Instead of saying things such as, "I will never be successful because of the family I come from" or "God can't use someone like me," we begin to say, "I am more than a conqueror in Christ Jesus; I can do all things through Christ who strengthens me."

Our words create powerful atmospheres. When we fill our lives with words of defeat, fear, and weakness, then we live in a realm of dark bondage. When we fill our lives with God's words and His ways, then we create an atmosphere of faith, glory, and power where *all things are possible*.

When the enemy draws us back to old habits and sinful behavior, he wants to ensnare us and bind us in defeat. Most of the time if we make a mistake, there is so much guilt and shame that we tend to avoid the presence of God. It is the same type of flawed logic that gripped Adam and Eve in the garden when they hid from God—as if it is even possible to hide anything from the One who knows your every thought, cell, weakness, and strength! Thus the enemy tries to falsely place a barrier between us and God.

But Jesus shed His blood for us and reunited us with our Father:

> But Christ, when He came as a High Priest of the good things to come, by a greater and more perfect tabernacle, not made with hands, that is to say, not of this creation, neither by the blood of goats and calves, but by His own blood, He entered the Most Holy Place once for all, having obtained eternal redemption.
>
> —HEBREWS 9:11–12

Our call is to live as the sons and daughters of the living God. We are not created to live as beggars but as priests and kings. God has made a way for us to come boldly before His throne.

When we stumble, we are actually instructed by God to run directly to Him. We are to receive His grace in our time of need. His love draws us away from the bondage and into freedom.

OLD BONDAGES CREEP BACK IN

Early in my ministry God gave me an assignment for young people, and I hosted an annual youth camp. Our meetings were so rich with the power of God. I witnessed moves of God that blew my natural mind. I remember one time when I was preaching and waved my hand and the whole front row slid out of their seats under the power of God! There was rich glory in that place. One of the young men had been battling extreme rebellion. God encountered him that day and cleansed his heart. Those camps became places of supernatural deliverance and miracles. It was a very special time in my early ministry.

I do not host these youth camps anymore, but they were life changing when we had them. They became known as meetings where God put broken young people back together and melted the hardest hearts. One year I received a heartbreaking call about a young man who was severely bound with sexual addiction on a level that few people can comprehend. He told me stories that turned my stomach and confounded my mind.

We prayed for him and immediately broke the power of the devil. I assigned a prayer team to meet with him. We poured both faith and anointing into him. Within the first couple of days we saw transformation. As the week went on, there were major changes in his demeanor in every way. God was transforming this young man and revealing Himself to him. By the time that young man returned home, he had experienced major deliverance. His mom called to tell me how different he was and how excited she was. He continued to live as a transformed man! I was so thankful for what the Lord had done and that I could be a small part of His plan for this individual.

Months after the youth camp, I got a call from the young man's mother. She updated me about their family and how he was doing. She was so happy that he had not gone back into the kind of dark behavior that he was involved in before. He joined in on the conversation, and we had a good time catching up. I began to ask him some very simple questions about small behaviors: thought life, eye gates (what you see), ear gates (what you hear), and other personal behaviors. It was clear to me from his answers that he had let his guard down and allowed some very small subtle deceptions to creep back into his life. In my experience, when a person comes out of a strong lifestyle of deception and bondage, they have to keep even the little doors slammed shut. I warned him and his mom that he needed to close those doors to maintain his freedom. They were unconcerned and felt that because he was not engaging in major failures, he was all right.

I could see what they couldn't; the little doors were leading to the bigger ones. Over time the enemy was drawing him back into old patterns and bondages. To be transformed we have to learn to live transformed! This takes work and spiritual diligence. Eventually he was dragged back down the same old path. This is the plan of the enemy, to steal our freedom and bankrupt our deliverance. Opening up old wells of sin and bondage is one of his chief tricks.

No Time to Be Passive or Aimless

Author Neil T. Anderson states in his book *Winning Spiritual Warfare*: "You may be wondering, 'If my position in Christ is secure and my protection is found in Him, why do I have to get actively involved? Can't I just rest in Him and let Him protect me?' That's like a soldier saying, 'Our country is a major military power. We have the most advanced tanks, planes, missiles, and ships in the world. Why should I bother with wearing a helmet, standing guard, or learning how to shoot a gun? It's much more comfortable to stay in camp while the tanks and planes fight the war.' When the enemy troops infiltrate, guess who will be one of the first soldiers to get picked off!"[1]

I believe Anderson sums up the attitude of many Christians quite perfectly in this analogy. There are far too many who want to embrace a passive spirit and just hope that things work out. Some are even offended by the suggestion that we should have any awareness of the plots of the enemy.

The truth is that our high commander, Jesus, has not only fully equipped and armed us for victorious battle, but He has also entrusted us with navigating His plans and putting the enemy on the run! The Lord has provided effective battle strategies for His people and made every provision for our success. We cannot and must not yield to a false sense of lethargy. We must put on our armor, deploy our weapons, and skillfully execute the strategies of heaven. We fight not from a position of fear but from a high point of offensive victory.

The Apostle Paul made a strong point in his first letter to the Corinthian church when he declared that his own personal battles were not being navigated without intention and purposeful living:

> I therefore so run, not as uncertainly; so fight I, not as one that beateth the air: But I keep under my body, and bring it into subjection: lest that by any means, when I have preached to others, I myself should be a castaway.
> —1 CORINTHIANS 9:26–27, KJV

Paul said he consciously made a daily decision to put his flesh under his authority. His exact words are: "I keep under my body, and bring it into subjection." He was not referring to a one-time event. He did not state that in the past tense but in the present tense. He was talking about something he did on a regular basis. When you have been set free, then you must slam the doors shut on the enemy.

MAKING WISE DECISIONS

You live free and keep the flesh "under" by making wise decisions. You place great confidence in the delivering power of God and His absolute redemption in your life, but you do not leave wiggle room for the flesh. Many people have fallen into traps they never imagined would be possible in their lives. There are great preachers and effective ministers who are sidelined right now because of some bad decisions. They did not guard themselves against traps and snares.

Wisdom dictates that you walk and live differently from those who are unwise. I remember a time when I first went to Bible college. One of our male teachers, who was also a pastor, said that he never counseled a woman by himself. Another person would always be with him. He explained that it was wisdom to avoid any temptation or opportunity for his flesh to fail. I am positive that there are some ministers today who would give anything to go back in time and make some different decisions. We have to use wisdom and keep the doors slammed shut, not giving the flesh an opportunity. We have an opponent who does not play fair; Satan can and will use every weakness of your flesh to his advantage.

When shackles have been broken and bondages are removed, you keep yourself free by continuing to say yes to your spirit man and a loud no to your flesh. Paul goes on to say in 1 Corinthians 9:27 that he does not want to become a castaway. He does not want all of his labors to end in ruin because he succumbed to fleshly appetites. So he made a regular habit of crucifying his flesh and feeding his spirit.

Think about how profound this passage is when it's applied to the life of the Apostle Paul. This unique man had the strength to give himself fully to the gospel, never marrying, never having a family, and never giving in to the temptation of the flesh in that area of his life. He endured physical beatings for the cause of Christ. He was rejected by scores of people and attacked by many others. He was left for dead more than once. He was imprisoned and mired in human feces and urine, all because of his faith in Christ and his commitment to the gospel. Yet in those sufferings he walked so deeply with God that he was entrusted by Him to write two-thirds of the New Testament.

Did Paul consider himself a spiritual giant who was beyond the corrupting reach of his own flesh? No. Rather he said that he daily put his natural man under subjection. We cannot afford to think or feel that we are too spiritual or too mature to give in to the desires of our flesh. We need to heed the following profound advice of this spiritual father, Paul, and make wise decisions to slam the door shut on fleshly failures:

> Those who are Christ's have crucified the flesh with its passions and lusts. If we live in the Spirit, let us also walk in the Spirit.
> —GALATIANS 5:24–25

REJECT THE LURE OF THE PAST

We want to have longevity in the things of God. We want to complete the course. We want to fully execute our assignments.

When a person spends years of his life living in calamity, his mind develops horrible thought patterns that create fleshly appetites and cravings. If a person gives himself over to sinful desires on a repetitive basis, he will often fall prey to the influence of a demonic spirit.

For example, a young person is exposed to pornography at an early age. He grows up looking continually at unclean images and develops a deep fantasy life filled with lust. Eventually he begins to act on his desires. Over time he becomes bound by a spirit of lust and cannot seem to break free. Despite conviction and a strong desire to come out of the bondage, he is so entangled that he can't seem to break free.

This is the pattern of deception that unfolds in a person's

life if he is not set free by the power of God. The same process often unfolds with fear or rejection. The enemy sets a person up at an early age and reinforces his plans over a period of years. The person faces a trauma of rejection or fear and then develops a lifestyle of subjection to a false reality. God never called that person to live in the miry pit of fear or the sorrow of rejection. That person's mind embraces a distorted reality that clouds his judgment and damages his emotions.

I have seen so many men and women who are bound by extreme rejection. It constrains them and stifles the plan of God for their lives; it hinders their relationships and creates unrealistic expectations and fears. They grow up searching for love, but their battered souls actually crave wounds and rejection because they feel comfortable with those traumas!

They become drawn to people who feed their insecurities, and they have great difficulty engaging in healthy relationships because of their deep soul wounds. They develop emotional and mental strongholds that confine them. They self-protect and misread people who are sent into their lives.

A person bound by rejection needs the freedom of Jesus in order to have strong relationships and become an effective member of the body of Christ. It takes the healing power of God to set a person free from this type of condition.

A soul that is under siege will often retreat into the dark areas from which it came. During extreme stress and emotional turmoil it is easy for the flesh to embark on an old road. The attack plan of the enemy is to overwhelm, bombard, and bind up. He would absolutely love to take you back to the place you were before Jesus set you free.

Being drawn back to an old bondage is nothing more than a tactical lie from the enemy's camp. It is one of the identifying marks of the devil's dark plots against your life. You can recognize the ploys of the enemy and his schemes and break them with the power of the name and blood of Jesus and the Word of God. You do not have to surrender or accept any level of defeat.

Chapter Ten

ATTACK SYMPTOM 8—
QUESTIONING DIRECTION AND
CALL THAT WAS ONCE CLEAR

▼▼▼▼▼▼▼▼▼▼▼▼

O NE OF THE favorite tools of the devil is intimidation. As a spiritual attack unfolds, fear and intimidation are two of the strategies for defeat deployed by
demonic forces. To *intimidate* means "to make timid or
fearful: frighten; especially: to compel or deter by or as if
by threats."[1] Intimidation induces a sense of fear and infe-
riority, allowing the bully to take charge over the one being
intimidated. This tactic gives us some very clear insight into
the kingdom of darkness: the enemy operates as a spiritual invader, advancing into territory that does not belong
to him, roaming and prowling around looking for a small
crack he can enter through. When he gets a foothold, he then
unleashes his nonsense in an effort to take charge.

His minions ruthlessly execute an evil master plan
designed to release fear, intimidation, confusion, and shame
in order to stall out the progression of the amazing plans the
Father has laid out for each of us. But Jesus stripped the devil
of all legal authority over the life of a believer:

> And having disarmed authorities and powers, He made
> a show of them openly, triumphing over them by the
> cross.
> —COLOSSIANS 2:15

Jesus's triumph means that every time the enemy attacks, he is trespassing on God's property. He makes a lot of noise and does all he can to divert attention from the promise and onto the problem. He is the master of distraction. He loves to use smoke and mirrors to deceive us and turn our focus toward the wrong things. He does not want us to live with clarity or an abiding sense of purpose.

The Bible compares his actions to those of a lion:

> Be sober and watchful, because your adversary the devil walks around as a roaring lion, seeking whom he may devour. Resist him firmly in the faith, knowing that the same afflictions are experienced by your brotherhood throughout the world.
> —1 PETER 5:8–9

DO NOT UNDERESTIMATE THE ENEMY

The fierce roar of a lion can be heard up to five miles away![2] Even if you are far away from the "king of the jungle," you can easily distinguish his powerful sound among the others in the wild. At a close distance the roar is so powerful it will rattle the metal on a truck or car. When the lion roars, he is confirming his dominion in a territory. He is letting every other creature know that the territory is under his control. He is also alerting the other lions of his anger.

The roar is not intended to notify prey of an attack. On the contrary, when a lion attacks, it is silent. It moves in stealth mode to take out its prey with precision. There is no warning! The lion is a master predator and uses well-developed hunting skills to swiftly and suddenly devour prey.

The tremendous volume and unmistakable sound of the lion's roar also creates an atmosphere of fear. Sights, sounds, and imaginations create atmospheres. Atmospheres are powerful to unlock imaginations, ideas, feelings, and reactions.

The enemy employs the strategy of the lion and uses the power of sight, sound, and thought in an attempt to overtake the believer. He wants to create a toxic atmosphere filled with fear and questioning. He wants to paint a mental picture of defeat and failure. He wants to make the journey look so impossible that you just give up. This is his war strategy against you.

Of course, the reality is that the enemy's power over you and me was broken at Calvary. He roars and attacks in an attempt to get us into fear so that he can have a legal right to come in, but he has no rights to us unless we yield to him.

Like the hunting lion, Satan carries out his missions undercover and does not announce his attack plans. He camouflages himself and works hard to keep his presence hidden because the element of surprise provides a distinct advantage in the hunt. He maneuvers subtly—twisting, lying, deceiving, and confusing. He does not want to be exposed; he prefers to remain hidden so he cannot be conquered.

By concealing himself, he has convinced many people that he is not even real. He also gets many Christians to live in such a fleshly realm that they shun teaching and learning about the spiritual realm. It is almost mind-boggling to think that we get saved by believing in the miraculous ministry of Jesus, and then we are invited by some believers to just sink down into a world of mental comprehension void of any spiritual reality. I meet Christians all the time who don't even really think about or ponder the spiritual realm. They get upset if you talk about angels. They do not believe in radical miracles and unexplainable signs. I often wonder about this type of believer.

When you and I read the Bible, we read a book filled with stories that defy human understanding or logic. There are no nice and normal stories in the Bible. There are angels, demons, a God who created the heavens and the earth, and strange creatures and wonders. The Bible tells of many miracles, unexplainable healings, and illogical breakthroughs. God is not an idea or concept. He is a supernatural being, and we too are called by Him to live in the supernatural.

Satan would like nothing better than for us to minimize his tactics and operations. He would be thrilled if we just stayed in the dark and were unaware of what he was doing under cover. He would like that because it would disempower us, stalling out our faith to tear his works down.

Exposure is one of the first steps to deliverance. You cannot conquer something that has not been identified. You cannot cast out or break something you have not discerned. This is one reason the devil hates prophetic people, prophetic ministry, and the office of the prophet so much. Prophets expose the demon that is hiding in the corner of the room. They are spiritual warriors. A prophet operating fully in his call lives with spiritual eyes and ears wide open. He sees into the spirit realm and identifies the word of the Lord. He also brings much-needed clarity and exposure to the plots of the enemy.

WALKING WITH GOD

Each believer is invited to live in the realm of spiritual insight. When you were born again, you gained full access to all that heaven has for you. You were not created to stumble around in darkness but to live in illumination and insight.

Though he operates much of the time under the radar, the enemy has another evil method of striking. He unleashes lies, accusations, and evil imaginations in an attempt to intimidate. This is the warning we are given in 1 Peter 5:8, that Satan will release these in a roar in order to bind us and take us captive. He is looking for those who will cower in fear so he may devour them. He has not been given the legal right or authority; therefore he has to seek access through fear. This is why we are made aware of his tactics—so we can recognize and resist.

As we walk with God, surrendering to His ways and trusting in Him completely, He unfolds our individual pathway of destiny:

> Trust in the LORD with all your heart, and lean not on your own understanding; in all your ways acknowledge Him, and He will direct your paths.
> —PROVERBS 3:5–6

In the process we discover spiritual gifts and mandates that were placed in our lives before we were born. There is a very specific calling and appointment for each life, and God provides supernatural direction for each of us. He opens up the avenue that we are to travel and provides the light to see it.

A life of devotion to His Word unlocks the wisdom of God to identify and pursue your purpose:

> My son, do not forget my teaching, but let your heart keep my commandments; for length of days and long life and peace will they add to you. Do not let mercy and truth forsake you; bind them around your neck, write them on the tablet of your heart, so you will find favor and good understanding in the sight of God and man.
> —PROVERBS 3:1–4

Tremendous power is unlocked by a person who spends daily time with God. Many people face unnecessary struggles because they do not prioritize their spiritual lives. As a believer you are called to walk with God daily. You must set time aside to seek Him. Many are frustrated because they are not walking closely with God. They cannot see the path ahead of them because their spiritual eyes are filled with sleep instead of passion and vision. Quality time in the presence of Jesus builds spiritual strength and tenacity.

THREE KEYS TO SPIRITUAL SUCCESS

There are three pillars of devotion that are the master keys to spiritual success:

1. The Word (reading and studying the Bible)

2. Worship

3. Prayer

We were apprehended by God to love and be loved by Him. This is the highest level of our lives with God, to have relationship with Him. This is ahead of our calling or purpose. You will never properly discover or fulfill your life's mission without first building relationship with Him. He is your compass. In His presence clarity comes forth. In His presence direction comes forth. In His presence revelation bursts forth like a river. His presence is the key to your spiritual success and longevity. It is absolutely impossible to spend consistent time with God without seeing major spiritual growth.

The Word

Reading God's Word ministers peace to your inner man and clarity to your mind. God's Word is like medicine that flows over your entire being. When you study the Scriptures and ponder the Word of God, faith is built. A life that is hidden in the Word of God is full of revelation, peace, and spiritual strength. It is very hard for a person to be deceived when he knows the promises of God. God's Word will straighten out a twisted mind. The mind can be renewed by the Word of God. God thoughts are released, and a higher way of living is unlocked through time spent in the Bible.

Worship

Worship takes your spirit right into the throne room. Heaven is saturated in adoration, praise, and worship. We have to learn to manifest heaven on earth in our private time with God. We were saved not just to serve Him but also to have relationship with Him. Private worship and praise lift you far above this natural realm and into the presence of God. They empower you to live in victory daily. The life of intimacy is the life of destiny. Placing priority on devotion secures identity and spiritual success.

Prayer

Prayer is the intimate language of another realm manifesting now in this realm. Through prayer we become intimately acquainted with the person of Jesus. We pour out our hopes, dreams, and failures before God in prayer. We have an ongoing, unending conversation with the Lord in prayer. We tune in and listen to the Holy Spirit in the place of prayer. Daily time in the presence of God, through prayer, is critical. A person of prayer is also a person of great power.

The late revivalist Leonard Ravenhill summed it up this way: "A man who is intimate with God, is never intimidated by man."[3]

A strong spiritual life filled with God's Word, private worship, and prayer will arm you to win the battle against the devil's kingdom. You will be stirred up, fired up, and ready to storm the gates of hell. You will also have staying power when the ugly enemy shows up and unloads one of his vile attacks on you.

A Pastor Sets a Time Frame

A mentor of mine shared a story about a spiritual attack against a very sincere pastor. This pastor had gone with his wife, who was also a powerful preacher, and their family to a city. They went with one thing in mind, to build a great church that ministered to the city and transformed lives. God had given them so many wonderful breakthroughs. The building and property had come into their hands supernaturally. They had been given a beautiful facility that was perfect for the vision God had shown them.

They worked tirelessly in their pursuit of the vision but with only limited results. No matter what they did, they just could not seem to break through certain barriers and grow beyond a particular point. The pastor grew restless and frustrated. Frustration often leads to wrong choices and rash decisions. This is one of the breeding grounds for spiritual disasters.

The pastor was close friends with one of my mentors, who was a real powerhouse! This minister shot straight and said exactly what was on his mind. You did not ask this person a question if you did not want an honest answer. The pastor had called this mentor and stated that he decided that if something did not change within a certain time period, he would shut down the church and walk away. His desire was to see growth and a move of God within a certain time limit. Without hesitation my minister friend told the pastor that he might as well turn in his resignation and give up. He had just let the devil know that all he had to do was bombard that church for a certain number of days and he would win the battle! I understand that sometimes we have to make an honest evaluation of where we are. Sometimes one brook has dried up and there is another place of provision. This is why we must live tuned-in and be ready for new instructions. We must also realize that the purpose of the enemy's attack is to shake us loose from the assignment upon our lives.

The enemy was doing his best to defeat this pastor and shut down the church. The timeline was not something that heaven had declared, nor was it a word of wisdom. The pastor was questioning the call that he had received because he had grown extremely weary after a long battle. When my friend spoke so straight to him, it woke him up, and he shook off the confusion. Again, there are times when we must move on, but it will come to us with peace and clarity, not confusion and heaviness.

CONFUSION: THE ENEMY'S TRICK

The enemy loves to use confusion as one of his weapons. To be *confused* means to be "perplexed or disconcerted; disoriented; unable to understand or think clearly."[4] This is a picture of a mind under attack. It is unable to make a quality decision because reason is suspended by momentary trial. The waters of destiny suddenly become clouded as if they were a muddy pond instead of a swiftly flowing stream. A lack of clarity stops the forward motion.

Under the severe pressure of an ongoing attack, it is common to find yourself questioning the road you are traveling. The enemy creates confusion in the mind about divine direction and calling. His goal is to move you off the path of your destiny. He stirs the waters, plants negative thoughts, and releases discouraging reports. His aim is to incite fear and remove certainty.

You may begin to reexamine decisions that were previously crystal clear. The aim is to halt your progress and eventually push you backward. The enemy wants to mire you in the muck of heaviness and get you stuck. When you stop advancing, he piles on the pressure to get you to retreat. This is his battle plan.

God does not create or endorse confusion. He is not double-minded, nor does He speak in an unclear manner:

> For God is not the author of confusion, but of peace, as in all churches of the saints.
> —1 CORINTHIANS 14:33

It is the work of our enemy that pollutes the spiritual climate and makes it seem as if the will of God is unknown. Again, this is not the truth; it is the momentary situation created when the enemy rains down confusion in the midst of the attack. When your mind has been overwhelmed and bombarded for a long period of time, you become disengaged and search for relief. You are battle weary and just want to enjoy some solitude.

At such a time you are emotionally, even physically, vulnerable and must be on guard against deceit. It will not be overtly evident but subtle and cleverly devised. We see it in the way the devil deceived Eve. He used trickery and subtlety:

> But I fear that somehow, as the serpent deceived Eve through his trickery, so your minds might be led astray from the simplicity that is in Christ.
> —2 CORINTHIANS 11:3

Notice the devil did not come in and tell Eve what he was really planning for her. No, he came in with deception and wove a web that was based on lies. He is skillful in his operation and clever in his pursuit. He does not come and tell you that if you listen to him, your life will be shipwrecked. On the contrary, he comes and makes you a multitude of empty promises. He accuses you and bombards you with false guilt and then promises you peace even though his real plan is to release more torment.

FALSE LEADING AND FAMILIAR SPIRITS

Due to the enemy's trickery Eve's mind was led astray from the simplicity of loving God and believing His word to her. The major battle during an attack is in the mind. This is why it is vital that we renew our minds and walk in the Word. We will examine successful battle strategies in chapter 13. When the enemy continually harasses and confuses the mind of a person under attack, the person can lose his bearings if he is not firmly planted in the Word of God and secure in the prophetic declaration over his life.

I have seen people in the midst of an attack make a sudden and unexplainable course change. I understand that sometimes we miss it, get off course, and then must examine ourselves and change direction. However, we must be cautious about making a wrong decision in a time of trial.

During a time of spiritual upheaval the enemy can release a false leading. What do I mean by this? In John 10:27 Jesus tells us that His sheep hear His voice. When good sheep hear Him, they follow Him. They pursue the direction He is clearly laying out for them. There is never a time in our lives when we are to be stuck without direction. God continually leads and guides us. He speaks to us in many different ways: sometimes we hear an inner voice; other times we may have a prophetic dream or experience a vision; at other times prophecies may be given to us; or, often, we may receive revelation from His written Word. He is always speaking. We have to make a strong effort to tune in to what He is saying.

But during an attack God seems to speak less often and less clearly. It is during this tribulation that the enemy can strike with exceptionally heinous intent. As your mind is reeling from the various circumstances, and there seems to be a lack of emotional peace, he ups the ante. He comes in and withdraws some of the mental attacks and releases a false leading in their place.

Evil spirits of deception are called "familiar spirits" in Scripture. They are described as working with mediums to imitate the spirits of dead people:

> Regard not them that have familiar spirits, neither seek after wizards, to be defiled by them: I am the LORD your God.
> —LEVITICUS 19:31, KJV

I believe there are types of familiar spirits and other deceptive demons that can imitate the Holy Spirit in an effort to misguide God's people. When Satan tempted Jesus, he quoted Scripture:

> Then the devil took Him up into the holy city, and set Him on the highest point of the temple, and said to Him, "If You are the Son of God, throw Yourself down. For it is written, 'He shall give His angels charge concerning you,' and 'In their hands they shall lift you up, lest at any time you dash your foot against a stone.'" Jesus said to him, "It is also written, 'You shall not tempt the Lord your God.'"
> —MATTHEW 4:5–7

The devil was trying his best to separate Jesus from His destiny. He struck Jesus at the end of an extended fast and appealed first to His natural hunger. When that didn't work, he attempted to twist Scripture to deceive the wisest being in the universe. Jesus responded with the Word.

This account exemplifies a false leading. It was concocted

by the devil, and he attempted to disguise his true nature and plans in order to get Jesus off course.

When the devil comes to a person whose mind has been clouded, he can withdraw a measure of the emotional attack and allow a false sense of peace to take hold. Amid this temporary calm he has one of his minions release a false leading: a thought about taking a new direction, abandoning a post, or letting go of a particular truth. Many times the person will mistake the operation of this familiar spirit for the leading of the Lord because in the moment that it comes to him he is feeling a temporary relief from the battle.

The purpose of the false leading is to cause the believer to take a wrong course of action. This is why the attack unfolded in the first place, to move the person out of his destiny. The enemy can appear as an angel of light (2 Cor. 11:14) who does not show his true colors but instead paints a false picture to deceive his intended target.

Many times I have seen extremely gifted people removed from their calls and the direction God had for their lives because they yielded to the pressure of an attack. Their judgment became clouded, their minds weary, and their bodies tired. They listened to the wrong voice.

It is vital to know God's promises and stand on them. It is also important to have a record of the prophetic declarations that have been made over your life so that you remind yourself of the course Jesus has set for you. Having the right people in your life provides another much-needed safeguard. It is key to have people who will get down in the trenches to pull you out rather than wallowing around in the mud with you.

YOU DIDN'T COME
THIS FAR TO GIVE UP

If you find yourself questioning God's assignment on your life, stop and examine where you are and how you got there. Are you in the middle of an intense trial? Have you previously had peace and clarity about your purpose? If the answers to the above questions are yes, then the situation is clear: you are under an attack. The last thing you need to do in this moment is to make a hasty decision in an effort to get out of the line of fire. You will come to regret your retreat.

Go back and remember the joy you had when you discovered God's plan and what you were supposed to do. I am sure that in those past moments you had a pie-in-the-sky view of your call: you thought you'd be walking on a path that would be free from any adversity. But that view is just not real life! There are challenges that come as the plan unfolds. There are potholes in the road of destiny. These things refine us and sharpen us.

David did not get into the palace without first squaring off against Goliath. Paul received his apostolic call but was then sent into the desert. Jesus was led into the wilderness and had to tangle with the devil before beginning His ministry. Every champion passes through a storm. The storms only serve to confirm the calling. Do not let your momentary affliction overshadow your eternal destiny. It too shall pass.

Now is the time to remind yourself of the things God has already spoken over you. Get out your prayer journal. Listen to recordings of prophetic words that have been declared over your life. Do not turn the helm of your life over to another captain! Do not jump into a life raft to try to make an escape. If you find that you have loads of questions you did not have before this attack began, then that is just confirmation of where you are. Those thoughts are meant to take you out. They are sent to bring confusion to you and cause you to retreat. But this is not the hour for retreating; it is *not* that time.

Recognizing the work of the enemy empowers you to take bold action to resist it. It releases a spirit of determination on you to navigate these choppy waters with your assignment intact. A clouded picture of your purpose is nothing more than a cheap ploy of the enemy that pales in comparison with God's majestic plan for you. Stay on course. Stay rooted in the plan. Don't give up—you didn't come this far to give up. God is not finished yet, and there is a way forward.

Chapter Eleven

THE BATTLE OF THE MIND

▼▼▼▼▼▼▼▼▼▼▼▼▼

THE PRIMARY PLACE of attack is within the thought life. There is a great battle waging for the minds of human beings. Your adversary, the devil, has studied people for centuries and understands the creative nature of thoughts. He realizes thoughts are seeds that contain both creative ability and imagination. He wants to plant false seeds to unveil false destinies. He wants to overwhelm and bombard the mind with negative and fear-based accusations. He wants to establish deep soul wounds and mental strongholds that form a fortified fortress of deception and evil.

A spiritual attack will always involve the mind. It is therefore vital that we understand the power of our imaginations and thought lives. Part of obtaining the victory is uncovering the hidden truths regarding the power of thoughts. Much of the battle unfolds across the landscape of the human imagination.

We must begin with the understanding that the mind is the creative center of our beings. It is in the mind that we imagine future victories, create life-changing ideas, and remember the sting of past defeats. The inner thought life of a person can absolutely make or break his life. The destiny God has so meticulously planned hinges on the creative power of a renewed mind. A mind that is bogged down in old pain and wrong thinking will give birth to negative imaginations and pictures.

When a person is born again, he receives total forgiveness, absolute redemption, and kingdom authority. The human spirit is remade in the image and likeness of God. It now contains the DNA of the divine:

> For you have been born again, not from perishable seed, but imperishable, through the word of God which lives and abides forever.
> —1 PETER 1:23

When we are born again, we are born of the Spirit. We are created to live and move in the Spirit. There are simply no limits for the born-again man or woman. We are no longer limited to live by the dictates of our fleshly man or natural mind. We are like a bird let out of a cage, set free to soar. Every force that would confine us is broken, and we are powerfully reborn with the nature of our Father on the inside of us. We are no longer called to live our lives solely in the flesh but are created to move and dwell in the Spirit, unlocking limitless possibilities.

RENEWING THE MIND IS A PROCESS

Despite all the victory and redemption that was purchased for every Christian, there are still those who live far beneath God's glorious plans for them. Too many of God's children live way beneath their potential. In fact, a great many believers seem to live in a state of ongoing struggle and defeat. Their lives are like unique arrows in the hands of a skilled archer, yet they appear to miss the target. Why is this? One of the primary reasons is the presence of old mental bondages and the refusal to do the difficult work of renewing the mind.

Many believers mistakenly believe all their problems are going to disappear after they march to the front of a gathering and have someone pray for them. Don't get me wrong;

I believe in miracles. I believe God's power can instantly shift an entire life. I believe the presence of Jesus can totally heal cancer in a moment. I believe God can heal a family instantly. I have both seen and experienced God's mighty miracles. I love the miracle ministry, but the gift of an instant miracle is different from the process of renewing a mind and learning to live in the new reality of redemption.

Most people have grown up in situations that are contrary to the promises of God in some way. For example, maybe in your family people are more aware of sickness and disease than they are of the healing promises of God. Perhaps it is normal in your surroundings, when speaking of various illnesses, to say things such as, "Well, my grandmother had that, and I will probably get it too." Those are thought patterns that will ultimately serve to produce more faith in the problem than in the answer. They create spiritual realities that are contrary to the healing promises of God in your life.

A person who is stuck in such a cycle may get into prayer lines over and over again for healing and experience breakthrough, only to lose what he received. He may ask why his healing continues to be stolen from him. The answer is that he has a destructive mental bondage that needs to be broken, and it will not break during a miracle moment. His inner thought life needs to be cleansed by the Word of God and his mind redirected to align with God's promises.

In "The Key to Totally Transforming Your Life," an article for *Charisma* magazine, author and minister Lisa Bevere compares the renewing of the mind to the cleaning out of a closet: "Our minds, like our closets, can become cluttered—not by clothes that are in or out of season but by the patterns or trends of this world. These outfits, or thought processes, may look like they belong in our closets the first few years they take up residence there. But with the passage of time, they soon appear threadbare and out of sorts. They fit too tight or too loose, too long or too short. Unless our closets—our minds—are cleared out and reorganized on a timely and regular basis, we will not be able to test and apply God's truth to our lives."[1]

When we get saved, we must take hold of the Word of God and the systems of the kingdom to embrace an entirely different way of thinking and living:

> Do not be conformed to this world, but be transformed
> by the renewing of your mind, that you may prove what
> is the good and acceptable and perfect will of God.
> —ROMANS 12:2

Doing this takes aggressive and continual human effort. We must give our minds over to the study and reading of God's Word along with meditation, deep pondering, and consideration. When we see truth, we must then apply it and retrain our brains.

Renewing, in the verse quoted above, means "a renewal, renovation, complete change for the better."[2] This single scripture says there is a massive transformation available to the believer who gives himself over to the process of renewing his mind. In fact, an unrenewed mind has the potential to shipwreck the spiritual destiny of a person. But the Bible declares that a man or woman with a renewed mind will successfully navigate the will of God. This also means that a person without a renewed mind may never fully apprehend the will of God for his life.

INNER THOUGHTS
DETERMINE OUR COURSE

Our inner thoughts determine the outer course of our lives. If we can get this reality planted deep in our consciences, then we will be on a pathway to personal growth and change. As long as we place the blame elsewhere and refuse to accept any responsibility for the negative thoughts we allow to remain lodged in our heads, our progress will be paralyzed. We have to grab the reins of our emotions and thought lives and make a determination that we will not stay the same. We will refuse to allow our minds to keep thinking thoughts that are contrary to the Word of God. We will not allow old soul wounds to remain hidden beneath the surface without being confronted by the Word of God. We will not allow false emotional walls to remain intact. We will not allow fearful thinking to dominate our thought lives. No longer will we remain in mental captivity. No longer will we be passive on the journey that is our own lives.

We have been given impressive weapons for strategic battle and advance. They are not natural weapons, because we do not face an enemy that lives, moves, and dwells only in the fleshly realm. Our enemy is one who operates in the spirit realm:

> For the weapons of our warfare are not carnal, but mighty through God to the pulling down of strongholds, casting down imaginations and every high thing that exalts itself against the knowledge of God, bringing every thought into captivity to the obedience of Christ.
>
> —2 CORINTHIANS 10:4–5

We have been fully armed and equipped to fight the fight of faith and come out on the other side with the prize.

We should not be in a state of continual retreat. So many Christians view spiritual warfare as a defensive fight, a one-sided activity in which they are continuously crouching down behind their shields of faith, dodging the fiery darts of the wicked one. We have been given offensive weapons to lay siege on the powers of hell. One of the greatest joys of our lives should be wreaking havoc on the enemy. The devil ought to tremble when a blood-bought child of God gets out of bed in the morning. The church has been radically sanctioned to win.

FALSE THOUGHTS CREATE STRONGHOLDS

We have been empowered by God, the Creator of the universe, to pull down mental strongholds. This is one of the most vital keys to our victory, at both the individual and corporate levels. The vivid reality is that even with all the blessing and backing of heaven, we will not overcome the enemy to receive the full harvest in our lives without tearing down the false system of thought patterns that exist.

A believer can go to church and learn about the love of God, receiving revelatory teaching, yet still struggle to believe that God truly loves him. How can this possibly be? After all, the Word is going forth, and he is hearing it. How can he remain the same? He can stay stuck in the trap of deception and confusion because there is a mental stronghold on the inside of him that is blocking the power of the revelation. The walls of this stronghold are made up brick by brick of false thoughts that form a massive internal fortress of confusion and pain.

A stronghold develops in the mind and emotions over time. It starts with a negative experience, an emotional pain, or a wrong imagination. Thoughts form as the person ponders the particular memory or imagination. As the mind keeps thinking on that thing, it paints a vivid picture. If this process continues, an entire way of thinking is formed. One reason the enemy goes after the mind so strongly is that he understands it is the center of creativity.

You have heard it said that a picture is worth a thousand words. In effect, that means when you see something, your mind has the capability of completely understanding what is being conveyed. Mental pictures are called imaginations. This is how the creative process works: the mind thinks on something, and that process forms an inner picture or imagination.

We know we have been created in the image and likeness of God (Gen. 1:27). God has many dimensions, one being that of Creator. Ultimately everything that exists, whether past, present, or future, is from the imagination of God. He created all life and authored the known universe. He brilliantly created and established all we have ever seen and all we ever will see. His mind contains a vast collection of images that ultimately became realities by His design.

He has bestowed that same creative ability in mankind. Music that captures a moment, a movie that fascinates a generation, and an impressive skyscraper designed by a brilliant architect all began as a single imagination. An imagination gives birth to a concept in the mind's eye. It creates a mental picture of a possibility.

The human mind was created as a canvas to be painted on with all the limitless possibilities of God. When you are contending for a fulfilled promise, it is the imaginations of your faith, the dreaming, and seeing the potential that give images to your belief. God employs the mind's eye to allow you to see the promise. The prophetic spirit often releases powerful visions of spiritual reality to our inner man. Imaginations fuel potential.

Many times the enemy declares defeat over us by simply releasing a negative thought. He wants us to give life to that thought and water the dark seed it contains. When we ponder the evil thoughts planted by the enemy and allow the mind's eye to create pictures of gloom and defeat, we fuel our own failure. This is one of the great internal struggles—to keep our minds fixed on the right things and to cut off evil influences.

Each and every thought is a seed that contains a possibility. The growth of that seed is dependent on the soil it is planted in and the nurturing that is supplied. One key to successful spiritual warfare is governing the thought life by the Word of God and recognizing the enemy's invading thoughts.

A number of years ago I had an encounter that illustrated the reality of mental warfare. I was talking with a person who had suffered from extreme emotional torment for years. Suddenly my spiritual eyes were opened, and the discerning of spirits was activated. I actually saw the spirit that was causing this person so much trouble. It looked like an ugly little furry creature that was wrapped around the person's head with its mouth at the person's ear, and it was continually whispering tormenting and confusing thoughts.

Recently I had another similar experience. A young woman who was in one of my meetings was being prayed for by an intercessor. The woman needed to be set free. Suddenly I saw a vile little creature buried in the woman's chest. It was mocking God, mocking the prayers being prayed, and spewing lies that were lodging in the woman's mind and keeping her out of victory. The foul imp had the poor woman bound and deceived. I could see it so clearly. It was not the woman, but it was the spirit that had a grip on her that was perpetuating her bondage. It did not want to let go. If our spiritual eyes were open every day, we would be shocked to see all the spiritual traffic around us!

These two experiences further validate the reality of actual demonic spirits that come against the mind. If we as believers can discern and cast down thoughts that are in seed form, then we can keep them from becoming lasting imaginations.

THE PATHWAY TO VICTORY

Imaginations are like inner movies that play out a possibility. If, when the enemy invades a person's thought life with a wrong thought, he does not take authority over it and cast it down, it develops a root system. This system then breeds images in his mind's eye. That is how the creative system of our intellect works. It begins with a single thought. When this thought is watered and fed, it becomes a series of images (imaginations, dreams). Over time this thought then forms a stronghold that develops a pattern of behavior. Outward behavior becomes a living reflection of inward thought life.

First Peter 1:13–16 gives us firm instructions on how to secure a victorious pathway. We are told to "gird up the loins," which are the reproductive centers of our minds. This passage confirms the fact that our psyche is the creative part of our being:

> Therefore gird up the loins of your mind, be sober, and rest your hope fully upon the grace that is to be brought to you at the revelation of Jesus Christ; as obedient children, not conforming yourselves to the former lusts, as in your ignorance; but as He who called you is holy, you also be holy in all your conduct, because it is written, "Be holy, for I am holy."
>
> —1 PETER 1:13–16, NKJV

The literal picture here is of a person wearing flowing garments and tucking them in carefully at the belt line. We are being instructed to tie up the loose ends and remove the opportunity to stumble over wrong thought patterns, imaginations, or ungodly strongholds. There is tremendous potential and energy contained in the thought life. When our minds are renewed and partnering with our redeemed human spirit, we access the unlimited dreams of our Father God and tear down the impossibilities. We release powerful dreams and visions. We begin to see the possibilities and imagine the victories.

We are called in this passage from 1 Peter to have a "sober" mind, one that has not been intoxicated and numbed by false thoughts. Many believers are numb to the things of the Spirit because their minds and imaginations are so full of other things. They have not been dreaming God's dreams, pondering His will, or chewing on His Word. They are consumed with all kinds of thoughts that are contrary to His Word. This state of mind acts as an intoxicating force that hinders them.

But as the thought life is secured, the spiritual senses are empowered and the level of discernment is sharpened. We see the focus of our lives move from our intellects to our behavior. When our minds are placed on the proper course, our pathway is unobstructed, and our feet are swift to run with God's appointed destiny.

SOUL WOUNDS THWART DESTINY

Another issue that we must confront in our quest to live free is "soul wounds." Many people are doing their best to discover and accept the will of God for their lives, but there seems to be a barrier that blocks their success. They struggle with particular behaviors, attitudes, and actions that contaminate their obedience and undermine their relationships. Despite a real commitment to the plan of God, they keep stumbling. This can be the fruit of a wounded soul.

A soul wound is an emotional hurt that has not been addressed. It is a part of the mind that is infected and desperately needs healing. In the hands of the enemy a soul wound, even one inflicted long ago, can easily be used as a current tool to perpetuate an ongoing spiritual attack.

All of us have been designed by God as three-part beings—spirit, soul, and body. Our mind, or our intellect, is a part of our soul. We do not consist of just one part. We are a spirit, we live in a body, and we have a soul, as Hebrews 4:12 (AMPC) illustrates:

> For the Word that God speaks is alive and full of power [making it active, operative, energizing, and effective]; it is sharper than any two-edged sword, penetrating to the dividing line of the breath of life (soul) and [the immortal] spirit, and of joints and marrow [of the deepest parts of our nature], exposing and sifting and analyzing and judging the very thoughts and purposes of the heart.

The Greek word for "heart" in this passage is *kardia*. It means "heart, the emotional center of our being, and the capacity of moral preference."[3] It is the part of us that produces desire and makes us tick. It is the inner part of our minds where decisions are made. The *heart* is the part of each of us that defines who we are.

In light of these definitions it is easy to understand why the adversary would like to attack our hearts, the inner mind we each have, and pollute it with wounds. Many times the enemy will use an old, unrecognized, and unresolved emotional wound as a gateway for a present attack. It is possible to experience hurt and bitterness about something that is going on in your life right now that stings because of an old and unresolved soul wound. The devil loves to put his hand on a soul wound and dig in a traumatized area of the human mind. He uses those old wounds to perpetuate a false belief system and fuel his lies.

How does a soul wound develop? Typically there is a point of trauma that creates systems of thought and cycles of behavior. For example, a small child is abandoned by a parent. The trauma of rejection is released into the emotional or mental heart of that child. The incident creates a negative emotional wound that is often reinforced by other events. Over time the wounded soul creates a stronghold of fear and rejection that further creates polluted imaginations, false expectations, and unrealistic demands. As the wounded soul lashes out against people, relational misfires occur that create even more rejection and wounds. Walls begin to develop, and there is a pattern of unhealthy relationships established.

The soul wound drags the person down a path of continued defeat. His life moves in the opposite direction of his prophetic destiny. He has inner emotional turmoil that ultimately manifests in dramatic outer behavior.

Have you ever seen someone who thrives on constant drama? He may even say things such as, "I hate drama!" Yet all of his friends are emotionally unhealthy, he dates people who are unhealthy, and he creates dramatic situations on a regular basis. This is a prime example of an extreme soul wound. The person lives out what he knows, and what he knows is turmoil and drama. His inner self is not at rest. Until the wound is recognized and the healing flow initiated, he will remain under siege.

Finding Healing
From Soul Wounds

One key reason people are not healed of soul wounds is that though we are quick to identify the behavior, we don't deal with the root of the behavior. For example, a person may recognize that he continually has relationship issues, but what he's seeing is the fruit, not the root. He may see that he lashes out quickly in anger and may even identify an anger problem in himself, but again, the focus is on behavior. The deeper question he needs to ask is, "Why do I feel angry so often?" Revealing the soul wound opens the door for healing.

To be healed and set free you have to go on the journey of asking yourself: "What is the wound? How did it come into being? What doors need to be closed?" This is where it gets messy; the answers may point to something that doesn't always lend itself to a quick fix. You cannot always just run forward for a quick prayer and get everything resolved.

Many times an intentional step toward healing must be taken, and a whole new way of thinking must be discovered. You have to start processing information and experiences differently. That is work! But you will find that it is worth it when you are able to enjoy a life that is planted in peace and your soul is dwelling in Jesus.

When you begin the journey of healing, asking the difficult questions and giving honest answers, then you invite the healing power of God on the scene. Jesus loves to heal our minds. In fact, He has already paid the full price for us to live in complete and total peace:

> But [in fact] He has borne our griefs, and He has carried our sorrows and pains; yet we [ignorantly] assumed that He was stricken, struck down by God and degraded and humiliated [by Him]. But He was wounded for our

transgressions, He was crushed for our wickedness [our sin, our injustice, our wrongdoing]; the punishment [required] for our well-being fell on Him, and by His stripes (wounds) we are healed.

—Isaiah 53:4–5, amp

The word *sorrows* in this verse translates to "grief, pain, or sorrow [affliction]."[4] The good news here is that when Jesus shed His blood, He carried our inner pain and wounds so that we don't have to! He paid the absolute price for our emotional redemption. The enemy sees a gigantic "Off Limits!" sign on our minds. That sign is for him! He is not legally granted access to our souls. We can kick him out and initiate the life-giving flow of healing! We are boldly invited by Jesus to cast *all* our cares on Him (1 Pet. 5:7).

The divine peace Jesus paid for us to have is one of the wonderful gifts He ministers to us as the Good Shepherd. The Bible says He leads us to a place of peace and inner healing:

> The Lord is my shepherd; I shall not want. He makes me lie down in green pastures; He leads me beside still waters. He restores my soul; He leads me in paths of righteousness for His name's sake.
>
> —Psalm 23:1–3

Our lives were never meant to be tossed to and fro with inner pain and confusion. As we discover wounds in our emotions, we can put a demand on the healing ministry of Jesus. Just as the woman with the issue of blood jumped up from her bed of affliction and touched Jesus (Mark 5:25–34), so can we. We can rise up and worship the Healer, inviting Him into our emotions and pulling on the anointing of healing that rests mightily on Him.

How? You put a demand on His healing power! You begin to declare healing over your mind and speak the Word of

God. With the Holy Spirit's help you identify unhealthy routines and patterns. I recognized a soul wound in my life a number of years ago and embarked on this process. God's healing power began to flow right away. When I would spot that behavior, I would say to myself, inwardly, "OK, you are healed, and you are not going to act that way!" Then I would make my flesh line up with my promise. You have to learn to live and think like a healed person. This absolutely slams the door shut on the enemy.

A renewed mind—a healed and restored soul—is one that can soar far above the fleeting strategies of hell. Recognizing the pathway to peace and choosing to confront old soul wounds have the potential of unlocking another dimension of victorious living. These actions are of utmost importance in breaking spiritual attacks. You must confront the enemy's lies in your mind and release the healing power of God.

Chapter Twelve

THREE TYPES OF
COMMON ATTACKS

▼▼▼▼▼▼▼▼▼▼▼▼▼

T HE ENEMY HAS many different strategies in his war room. He uses a variety of weapons to bring frustration, confusion, and an overwhelming desire to just give up. In this chapter I will dig further into three very common types of attacks that we as believers face. The point in identifying these tactics is to equip you to fight them and win. As we have already discussed, you are not an accident; you were born, as Queen Esther was, for such a time as this:

> If you remain silent at this time, protection and deliverance for the Jews will be ordained from some other place, but you and your father's house shall be destroyed. And who knows if you may have attained royal position for such a time as this?
>
> —ESTHER 4:14

Esther was made queen for a precise moment in Jewish history! She was born for that moment in history, for she was the answer to the prayers of a generation. Her life was mapped out, each step leading to a moment of miraculous deliverance and extravagant favor. Her life is an example for all of us of many powerful lessons. One of the primary things we can recognize in her story is that her purpose was connected to the deliverance and freedom of many people.

Not everyone is tasked with as significant an assignment

as Esther was, but each of us has our own unique road to travel, and our obedience is directly connected to the lives of others. The soccer mom who fulfills a mandate to raise her kids in the fear of the Lord leaves a tremendous generational legacy. The small-business owner who dedicates his entrepreneurial endeavor to the Lord may fund the dream of a young prophet in his town who ends up ministering to countless people. Each dream is connected to other people's lives. Each assignment carries significant weight in the kingdom. We believe falsely that we will be rewarded based on the size of our gift and the reach of our influence. This is simply untrue.

When we examine the parable of the talents in Matthew 25, we see that rewards were based on stewardship. Jesus commended each servant's faithfulness to handle what he had been given. The servants were not rewarded based on how large their talents were but on how they managed them. I am convinced that some of the most celebrated people in heaven will be those who were unknown on this earth. I can't wait to see the intercessors receive their rewards!

JUST SAY YES

What the Lord is looking for from you and me is for us to say, "Yes!" He wants us to accept our assignments. We are often paralyzed by our own lack of confidence and a negative self-image. We think in our hearts, "I can't do this!" But that is exactly why you were chosen. Because *you* can't do it. He doesn't want you to do it in your own strength; He wants you to rely on Him. It is all part of this amazing process called life. We discover who God is and are awakened to the vastness of His being. We are then bathed in His unfailing love and grace. As we move deeper into the revelation of our redemption and inheritance, we are activated to our purpose. We find out that we are here for a reason.

Will we mess it up? Yes, we will. That is what grace is for. Will we feel overwhelmed at times by our own human limitations? Yes, but God is faithful, and His ability inside of us is rich. I was talking with a friend recently and sharing about a personal transition I have been navigating. I told him the Lord was asking me to step into unknown territory, that I was being stretched, and that the journey was challenging to me on many levels. I told him I was having to press in deeper to the Father in order to get my bearings. My friend shared a simple but deep truth with me. He said, "You can't grow without change."

If we are changing, then we are growing. Playing it safe will cause you to sit on the sidelines and dream about the what-ifs while others enjoy the exhilaration of actually being on this field called life. Choose not to waste the moments. If you fail, God will pick you up! If you run out of ideas, heaven has more. If you become maxed out, God will show you what to cut loose. Just don't sit, settle, and stagnate.

THE POWER OF A PROPHETIC PROMISE

Along the way the Lord will provide the road signs marking your journey and leading to the destination. He will give you prophetic pictures. He will speak to you in your private time with Him. He may give you prophetic dreams or night visions. He will minister to you through prophetic leaders. Each prophetic promise you receive has several aspects, but we will concentrate here on three of the most significant:

1. *It contains potential.* When God speaks to you, there is a vast amount of possibility based on your own choices and stewardship of what He has declared. Many people falsely believe that if God tells them something about their

lives, then it will come to pass with no effort
or response from them. I do not believe this
at all. I look at the lives of men and women in
the Bible and see that their pathway was most
often determined by their response to the word
of the Lord. Saul was never intended to die as
a rebel on the battlefield, void of the presence
of God. That was a result of his failure to obey
God. We can abort the power of the promise
with our own inaction and disobedience.

2. *It contains process.* Most of the time a prophetic picture points you toward the future.
   Prophets are described as forerunners in
   Luke 1:17. The prophetic spirit lives out ahead,
   beyond the confines of human time. Prophetic
   people see the future! They dream about what
   is yet to come. I believe the majority of prophetic people go to heaven with a heart that
   is full of dreams. Why is this? Because their
   spiritual eyesight allows them to see ahead.
   They discern things that are not only for their
   appointed times but also for the generations
   coming after them. Each time God speaks to
   our hearts about promise in our own lives,
   there is a process of development and prepa-
   ration to inherit the promise. It is usually not
   going to come the moment God says it. This
   is a prophetic principle that will save you lots
   of frustration. You must realize that the revelation of the promise is the beginning of the
   journey, not the end of it.

3. *It contains timing.* There is an appointed time for each promise. Promises will come to pass at the right moment as long as we cooperate with heaven. We do not have to get nervous or in a hurry. God is neither nervous nor concerned. He has the whole thing mapped out. There are moments in our lives when the door of favor and promotion swings wide open. We must discern the season and step into it. Usually we will have already been prepared in the process that has unfolded. Prophetic leading and ministry always have timing elements attached. This is why we must be sensitive and develop patience along with our faith.

When we have received a prophetic leading and are moving forward in our destiny, there is an unlimited amount of potential that is unlocked. A believer who has been activated and awakened to destiny is a threat to the kingdom of darkness. What is hell's response to this? It launches a spiritual attack. We will look at three common types below.

ATTACK 1:
DELAY IN FULFILLED PROMISES

As believers our very lives hinge on the promises of God. We confess our sins and turn toward Jesus based on a promise (Rom. 10:9–10). We patiently wait for the return of the Lord based on a promise. We sow with expectation of reaping based on promises. We are people of promise.

The Word of God is our promise book. As we dive deep into the truths of God's Word, we begin to discover all He has for us and all He has created us to do. Our hearts and minds begin to align with His proclamation over our lives.

We break the bounds of limitation and begin to soar with expectation. The life-giving promises of God take root in our hearts and minds, bringing hope and restoration in every area. We no longer live under the shadow of old things, past failures, or mistakes. We are made new and released to dream again. Each and every blessing found in the Bible is to be taken personally as a promise to you and me. But those promises must be mixed with faith in order to bring the expected results:

> For the gospel was preached to us as well as to them. But the word preached did not benefit them, because it was not mixed with faith in those who heard it.
> —HEBREWS 4:2

Faith is not a passive spirit that just sits and waits. Faith responds. It is a bold spirit that takes action. When your heart becomes filled with faith, you are compelled to get up and move! When God spoke to Abraham, He told him to rise up and go forth. Faith creates kingdom momentum and heavenly progress.

Faith fearlessly acts on the Word of God. Faith demands action. When blind Bartimaeus heard that Jesus was passing by, he began to cry out as loud as he could. He was unwilling to remain bound by blindness. He had received a revelation that God was able to heal him, and he was determined to do something about it:

> Then they came to Jericho. And as He went out of Jericho with His disciples and a great number of people, blind Bartimaeus, the son of Timaeus, sat along the way begging. When he heard that it was Jesus of Nazareth, he began to cry out, "Jesus, Son of David, have mercy on me!" Many ordered him to keep silent. But he cried

out even more, "Son of David, have mercy on me!"
Jesus stood still and commanded him to be called. So
they called the blind man, saying, "Be of good comfort.
Rise, He is calling you." Throwing aside his garment,
he rose and came to Jesus. Jesus answered him, "What
do you want Me to do for you?" The blind man said to
Him, "Rabbi, that I might receive my sight." Jesus said
to him, "Go your way. Your faith has made you well."
Immediately he received his sight and followed Jesus
on the way.

—MARK 10:46–52

Bartimaeus's determination to get the healing that he
believed belonged to him is the mark of faith. Faith creates a
holy boldness that will cause you to step out. Notice that the
religious people of that day kept trying to shut Bartimaeus
up. Isn't it interesting that the very people who should have
encouraged his faith were the ones the enemy used to shut
down his pursuit of God? Don't be surprised if the devil
sends people to give you negative reports and discouraging
words as you pursue breakthrough in your life. As I have
matured in the things of God, I have learned to view those
situations as confirmation that I am in fact on the right track.
Why would the enemy send negative people to dissuade me
if he wasn't bothered by my pursuit? When I changed my
mind-set, I was freed from receiving the weight of discouragement the enemy was trying to put on me.

The enemy always uses people in your life to give voice to
unbelief and negativity. They will call you crazy for believing
the Word of God. They will say you are too radical and
should calm down. They will tell you all the reasons that
what you are believing for will not come to pass. Those are
the voices of doubt and unbelief, and they must be tuned out
and ignored.

Thank God that desperate Bartimaeus ignored the religious voices of his day. He just kept crying out to Jesus with a supernatural determination. He is an example of what happens when a promise lodges deep in your spirit: you are uncommonly motivated! You are unwilling to remain silent because the reality of the promise overtakes your own mind.

While faith demands action, it also does not wear a watch. It does not look at the chronological passing of time and get discouraged because the breakthrough has not yet manifested in the natural realm. No, faith sees the thing as done and rests in the belief that the promise will come. It understands that heaven has perfect timing:

> We do not want you to become lazy, but to imitate those who through faith and patience inherit what has been promised.
> —HEBREWS 6:12, NIV

Attacks of weariness are launched at people who feel as if they have been standing and believing for a long time but are not yet seeing the results. The goal of the enemy during this type of an attack is to overwhelm the mind with negativity and pull a person outside of faith, beyond the realm of the spirit, to abort the promise before it comes to manifestation. It is key that the attack is discerned and broken. The person under assault must refuse to let go of his promise and must instead dig his heels in. Faith will bring the victory.

We are not to measure the promise by the passing of natural time. An attack of weariness comes to cause you to circumvent the process that is unfolding. It is intended to move your feet ahead of your character. We have often witnessed men and women who are filled with immense gifting but whose character has not been tried and developed through God's maturation process. When they are promoted, they end up crashing and burning for all the world to see. The kingdom of God does not need another crash-and-burn light show. It needs people who have been obedient to the process, whose characters have been firmly established, and whose steps are made sure.

It is during the process that we overcome personal weaknesses that could potentially shipwreck the promise. It is during the process that we confront self-esteem issues and internal doubts. This does not mean they don't ever crop up again, but during the waiting period they are revealed and refined. During this time our goal must be intimacy with God, not a particular achievement. It is amid the process that God calibrates our hearts and our minds to align with Him. Much is revealed during the waiting.

We must come to the understanding that the waiting time is precious. It is like the time period when the family is in the waiting room of a hospital anxiously anticipating the arrival of a new baby. We should have an excitement about the waiting! Not only is something coming, but also God is working in the waiting. I assure you: waiting time is not wasted time. Your obedience and response to the process will determine your next steps. Maximize the waiting time.

When I was in Bible college, instructors would tell us that we would eventually look back at our time there and realize how special it was. I knew it was a time that was rich with the presence of God, but I was chomping at the bit to get out of the starting gate and run my race. I must confess I have always struggled with waiting. I try to rush forward only to discover that I must surrender to divine timing. After I graduated and was in ministry and being hit by the enemy's missiles right and left, I looked back at my training time and recognized the value it held. The process prepared me for the promotion and the positioning.

For all of us there are times and seasons in our individual and corporate destinies. One of the assignments of prophetic people is to properly discern the times and seasons. In 1 Chronicles 12:32 we read about the sons of Issachar, a prophetic company in Israel that rightly understood times and seasons. I believe there is an Issachar anointing available for us today.

Every new season is framed with prophetic revelation. God speaks and reveals the season to us. He gives us revelation about the time we are in and the purpose of that time. We must understand that every promise and every vision has a proper time in which it is to be fulfilled. When God spoke to Habakkuk, He said the vision was for an appointed time:

> For the vision is yet for an appointed time; but it speaks of the end, and does not lie. If it delays, wait for it; it will surely come, it will not delay.
>
> —HABAKKUK 2:3

We will reap if we do not give up! The spiritual attack comes in an evil attempt to get us to give up:

> Be not deceived. God is not mocked. For whatever a man sows, that will he also reap. For the one who sows to his own flesh will from the flesh reap corruption, but the one who sows to the Spirit will from the Spirit reap eternal life. And let us not grow weary in doing good, for in due season we shall reap, if we do not give up.
>
> —GALATIANS 6:7–9

Verse 9 declares that there is a due season, an ordained moment of fulfillment. In the Greek the word for "due season" is *kairos*. It means "the right or opportune moment."[1] It is the supreme moment, a limited period of time, a time marked and pregnant with potential. It is the moment that what has been promised suddenly and swiftly comes into fruition. Each time God speaks a promise, there is a *kairos*, an ordained moment of fulfillment connected to the promise.

When the enemy is attacking and trying to get you to give up, you must bind him. Get out your promises and remind yourself of the words of the Lord. Refuse to back off from what God said. Hold on to it like a bulldog clinging to a bone.

ATTACK 2: DISCOURAGEMENT OVER SMALL BEGINNINGS

Each assignment begins in seed form. No assignment ever erupts in full force. Rather, assignments come with small beginnings and require our prayers, obedience, and faithful stewardship. Every great thing begins with a simple instruction. This is why we must live our lives tuned in to the voice of God with a heart that is ready to obey Him. Do not make the foolish mistake of measuring your destiny against the life of another person.

What do I mean by this? I mean that neither you nor I can run someone else's race. None of us can compare the destiny that is ours to that of another man or woman. Making the comparison will quickly open the door to great frustration and possibly toxic disobedience. God deals with us on an individual basis and has a personal destiny that is hand-crafted for each one of us.

The enemy works tenaciously to bring discouragement because the thing we are currently doing looks smaller than the thing we were born to do. In this type of attack the adversary releases warfare in the mind. He pulls levers of old wounds and rejections. He whispers into our ears that what we are doing is meaningless and pointless. He employs various tactics to bombard and overwhelm the mind and emotions. It is a deceptive attack meant to get us out of sync with the timing and the purpose of the Lord.

Many times people are carrying greatness but living in the wilderness. This paradox confounds the human mind. It stirs the thought: "How can I be headed for greatness when I am stuck here in the wilderness?" The kingdom of God is often marked by things that appear to be backward, actions that require a submission of the flesh to the spirit. In His kingdom we don't push our way forward; we serve our way ahead. The sayings of Jesus are challenging to the flesh and contrary to human thinking.

This is what stewarding the little things looks like: it comprises actions that often appear *backward* to us (and to others). It is the embrace of the kingdom of God above our own mental reasoning. It is putting our hands to something that seems small and insignificant to us yet finding that God places great value on it. On the journey to fulfilled purpose there will be many days of stewarding things that others deem unimportant and irrelevant. At the end of the day your success as a son or daughter is rooted in pleasing the Father, not gaining human approval or acceptance.

I am confident that David felt unimportant during the season in his life in which he was stuck tending to sheep. His father didn't get him; his brothers didn't get him. He was in the fields while they were off doing battle against enemies men deemed to be great and powerful. God needed to crush the spirit of ambition and man-pleasing in David before He released his full purpose. Those were being worked out in the process as He helped David come to the place where all his acceptance and joy came from the presence of God alone. He required a high level of surrender in David so He could launch him into a high level of purpose. The "little things" were actually huge in the developmental course God had laid out for David.

Greatness doesn't come overnight. It comes in small doses. It comes in daily routines. It comes through a series of right decisions. Great leaders advance while others give up. Great seers look beyond the picture everyone else is painting and identify something no one else sees.

David was locked out, rejected by his elders, and alone— but God was at work in Him. He was training him in many ways. There in the wilderness, while enduring the sting of being misunderstood and traveling the lonely path of the misfit, David found his inner core. He discovered why he was alive! He understood he was created to worship God and birth a prophetic generation that would unlock great victories for Israel.

In the vast fields of the lonely wilderness, David found a way to lift up his wounded heart to God:

> O God, You are my God; early will I seek You; my soul thirsts for You, my flesh faints for You, in a dry and thirsty land with no water.
> —Psalm 63:1

David sang the songs of worship and tapped into the reality of who he was: a prophetic worshipper who would lead a nation to unparalleled victory. The wilderness was training David. He would eventually face and defeat Goliath, the reviling enemy of Israel, but first he would face and take down the lion and the bear, the enemies of his father's flock:

> Your servant slew both the lion and the bear. And this uncircumcised Philistine will be as one of them, because he has reviled the armies of the living God.
> —1 Samuel 17:36

David pointed back to his experience in the wilderness to prove to King Saul he was qualified to take on Goliath. There is always a season that demands we steward something much smaller than what we have seen with our spirit eyes. It is in that season of small beginnings that our hearts are proved and our character refined.

It is also in the wilderness season that the voice of the accuser hurls lies at us. The enemy wants to attack and get us to bow to frustration and discouragement. We must remain vigilant and be faithful to what God has placed in front of us. If we cannot be trusted to properly steward the small thing, then why would God promote us?

The key to victory over the enemy's attacks is to stay focused! Keep your eyes on the task(s) at hand and refresh yourself in worship. Promotion will come in due season and at the right timing, but until then the most important thing is to keep your hands on the plow.

ATTACK 3:
BETRAYAL AND LONELINESS

One of the key ingredients of destiny in our lives is being connected with the right people. Relationships are imperative to God's plan for us. We must discern who the right people are and connect with them as God leads. I am a firm believer in ordained friendships, spiritual relationships, and divine connections. I remember what one of my mentors told me years ago. "Ryan," she said, "you need to decree glorious and divine connections every day." She had the revelation that relationships are critical to our spiritual success.

Strong relationships are rooted in commitment and honesty. A real friend loves you enough to speak the hard things to you openly and with your best interest at heart. One of the most devastating wounds you will ever face is a bitter betrayal by a trusted friend:

> Open rebuke is better than secret love. Faithful are the wounds of a friend, but the kisses of an enemy are deceitful.
>
> —PROVERBS 27:5–6

A betrayal is when someone who you thought had your best interest at heart and was loyal to you suddenly turns against you, striking you in an unexpected manner. Unfortunately in life and in ministry betrayal happens. Here in Proverbs it declares that the kisses of an enemy are deceitful. What does that mean?

This scripture is getting to the heart of betrayal. People with impure motives, operating in a wrong spirit, will use flattery as a tool to gain access to your life and heart. This is the entry point of many betrayals. Someone enters your life and appears to be a godly friend or associate, or represents some other type of relationship. He speaks to your soulish ambitions, telling you how great you are. The things he says sound kind, but there is an underlying spiritual influence at work.

David faced a devastating spiritual attack of betrayal through his own son Absalom. The story reveals one of the strategies the enemy keeps in his war room; it shows us the battle plan he uses in a betrayal. (See 2 Samuel 13–19.)

He first finds a person with an impure motive, usually someone who has his own internal wounds and is seeking to fill a void. Depending on what type of relationship you are dealing with, the void can be many different things. In the world of ministry relationships, an Absalom is usually a disgruntled leader.

Absalom was David's son. He was someone in covenant

with David. The enemy knows how to strike your emotions with maximum impact. He will go after someone who is close to you. This is why the gifts of the Spirit are so vital in our lives—God can reveal an impure motive before it ever manifests.

Absalom grew offended at David for the way he handled an injustice against his sister. He allowed the offense to drive a wedge between him and his father. Many believers allow wounds to fester and do not follow biblical counsel in confronting the person or people involved, which only increases the potential for disaster. Absalom began to rally people to his cause, but he did so in secret. An attack of betrayal hides under the cover of darkness.

I will never forget an attack I faced from an Absalom spirit. It tried to cut me to the core. The enemy used people I had trusted and relied heavily on in ministry. I believed they were in it with me for the long haul. The Lord visited me in a dream about one couple who was involved, giving me a clear warning about them. I approached them to inquire what was going on. They lied to my face while smiling at me and nodding their heads.

I am telling you, the enemy is ruthless. He creates a web of deception that invites people to break biblical protocol. He justifies the disobedience with an offense. Offended people will always gather together and share in the offense. This keeps them away from healing. Healing demands honesty and openness, but demons live in darkness.

Absalom was a man of great gifts. The Bible says he had absolutely no physical imperfection. He was completely perfect from head to toe. People were drawn to him just because of his looks. He used his attractiveness to rally others to take on his offense and join him in betraying King David. He launched a fierce attack against his father but ended up dying in a tree, snared and hung by his own hair, which was a sign of his beauty. The very gift God gave him was used by the enemy to exalt him in pride and then destroy him.

Everyone has gone through some type of personal betrayal. It may have been a dating breakup, a divorce, an affair, a church split, or a family member or friend turning against you. Scenarios such as these bring emotional pain and are designed to defeat and discourage.

What do you do in the midst of a betrayal? First you must make a quality decision not to stay wounded. Recognize that it is a spiritual attack. Make up your mind that you are going to pray and walk uprightly. You are not going to live in the past. There is nothing good to be found in the past. Refuse to get so comfortable with your pain that you just live there. Instead, press in for healing. Cry out to your healer! He is near to you and has healing for you. Bring your broken heart before the Lord and allow His healing virtue to flow. Get into His presence, pour out the pain, and allow Him to pour in healing balm. As you get into His presence, He will begin the healing process:

> The righteous cry out, and the LORD hears, and delivers them out of all their troubles. The LORD is near to the broken-hearted, and saves the contrite of spirit.
> —PSALM 34:17–18

The next thing you must do is make a decision to forgive. When I went through an awful Absalom attack, I sought the Lord for healing. He told me to begin to call out the names of my betrayers. Those people had stolen from me, wronged me, and acted like devils. The Lord told me to begin praying for them, declaring forgiveness, grace, and healing:

Bless those who curse you, and pray for those who
spitefully use you.

—LUKE 6:28

I didn't want to do that! I wanted to declare fire and wrath,
but God had other plans. When I first began to pray for them,
I could barely get the words out, but I made my flesh line up
with my spirit. As I pressed into that revelation over a period
of time, healing flowed to me like a river.

Loneliness is another form of spiritual attack that can be
an outgrowth of betrayal. The enemy loves to make you feel
as if nobody cares about you and you are all alone. He wants
you to have a pity party. The reality is that you are never
alone as long as you have Jesus. There may be times when
you have to be willing to walk without others, when it is just
you and Jesus, but that is all right. Don't give in to the feelings of loneliness. Keep an attitude of praise and thanks-
giving in your heart, and allow God to add the right people
to you at the right time.

Chapter Thirteen

FREEDOM FROM ATTACKS!

▼▼▼▼▼▼▼▼▼▼▼▼▼▼

N OW THAT WE have identified what spiritual attacks are, how they manifest, and the many different forms they take, it is time to put your faith to work and break the attacks. As has been established throughout this book, if you are born again, then you belong to God and are destined to be planted in the kingdom of light. You were not created to spend your life in constant struggle. You are a child of the King, empowered to win!

It is time to lace up your combat boots, grab the artillery, and put the enemy on the run. We are endued with heavenly power to combat the advancements of the enemy and send him packing.

KEYS TO BREAK AN ATTACK

Let's look at six keys to breaking a spiritual attack.

1. Break it with authority.

> Look, I give you authority to trample on serpents and scorpions, and over all the power of the enemy. And nothing shall by any means hurt you.
> —LUKE 10:19

We do not engage the enemy from a place of defeat. A lot of people miss it when they attempt to break an attack. They have a mental vision of despair and defeat. I have seen people try to beg God to break the attack. He has endued us with heavenly authority, and we are to use it.

If an armed robber came into your home in an attempt to steal your most valuable possessions and take things that had special meaning for you, how would you deal with him? Would you politely ask the intruder to leave? Would you beg someone else to enforce the authority to make him leave? Would you be passive about the situation?

Most people would rise up with great force and do all that was in their power to make the robber get out of their home and off their property. They would refuse to allow an invader to take things that were precious to them. They would not have to wonder about what they should do. Instinctively a normal person would rise up and fight with great strength.

The moment a thief steps onto your property, he tests your dominion. I doubt that you would be cautious in commanding him to leave. You would not second-guess whether or not he is in the wrong. No way! You would know with every fiber of your being that he does not belong on your property and is not authorized to take what is yours. That is a description of the spirit of dominion and authority in operation; you have a conviction that the boundaries of your physical property mark off a territory that is under your control.

In the same manner you must embrace a spirit of strength and authority concerning who you are in the spirit. When hell comes to plunder your family, your emotions, your body—or when any type of attack arises—you must meet it with strength. *Authority empowers strength.* The devil can smell weakness a mile away, like a shark being drawn to blood in the water. When the enemy hits you with an attack, he is looking, watching, and waiting for your response. If he hears timidity, then he knows he has a foothold. If he sees confusion, then he ramps it up. If he detects instability, then he knows he can keep bombarding. You have to come back at him full force.

You must lift up your voice and command him to take his hands off you! You break the attack with your words. As we learned earlier, words are keys that open and close spiritual doors. You use words of strength to tell Satan, "No!" A general does not ask the troops to advance. He *commands* them. In the same way you command the attack to be broken in the name of Jesus.

2. Break it with faith.

> Without faith it is impossible to please God, for he who comes to God must believe that He exists and that He is a rewarder of those who diligently seek Him.
> —HEBREWS 11:6

You break spiritual attacks with faith. Jesus told us that if we would only believe, then all things would become possible (Mark 9:23). Faith breaks through the barriers of limitation and opens up the realms of possibility. Faith receives the promise of God as already completed.

Faith is not rooted in a future tense. Hebrews 11:1 says, "Now faith…" Faith is a present help. Hope, however, points to the future. When someone says, "I sure hope that works out," what they are really stating is that they believe it could possibly happen in the future. Hope points to a possibility somewhere far off. Faith grabs the answer right now and begins standing.

Faith does not pray about mountains. Faith talks directly to the mountain (Mark 11:23). What does faith say? It says what God has already declared. Faith looks at a storm and speaks peace. Faith evaluates a sickness and declares healing. Faith observes adversity and boldly proclaims promise.

You break out of the limiting and constraining force of a spiritual attack by exercising your faith. Notice in Hebrews 11:6 that faith unlocks pursuit. Rewards are the result of pursuit. Spiritual attacks fail when we pursue the answer. As we call out to Jesus our deliverer and command the mountain to move out of our way, based on our promise, we unlock heavenly results.

3. Break it with prayer.

> Pray in the Spirit always with all kinds of prayer and supplication. To that end be alert with all perseverance and supplication for all the saints.
> —EPHESIANS 6:18

A lifestyle of prayer undoes the work of spiritual attacks. The Apostle Paul encouraged us in Ephesians 6:18 to live our lives in communion with God. What does that mean exactly? It means that regular, set times in the presence of God are absolutely key for us; each of us must establish and maintain them in our lives. In prayer we are strengthened. In prayer the mind of the Lord and the wisdom of God are unfolded to us. In prayer a strong assurance of the victory comes bursting forth like waters through a dam.

A strong prayer life will abort the assignment and the foul plots of the enemy. Prayer also releases much-needed wisdom strategies. When you recognize a spiritual attack, begin to seek God for His counsel and instruction. He already has the escape route mapped out and will lead you out with the spoils of the enemy.

4. Break it with resistance.

> Therefore submit yourselves to God. Resist the devil,
> and he will flee from you.
>
> —JAMES 4:7

The fierce winds of a spiritual attack blow aggressively in an effort to knock you down. It is very easy to just succumb to the pressure you feel mounting. That is exactly what the enemy is banking on. He believes that if he attacks you with great force, you will get tired and give up.

My spiritual father, Dr. Norvel Hayes, regularly stated, "The ministry of resistance is one of the greatest ministries in the Bible." What was he talking about? God gave you a wonderful ministry called *resistance*. It is a highly effective weapon of war against the powers of the enemy. You can resist your way right out of a temptation, and you can resist your way right out of a raging storm!

To *resist* means "to fight against; to remain strong against the force or the effect of (something); to exert force in opposition."[1] When we resist the bombardment of the enemy we are standing our ground and combatting him. We are embracing a fighting spirit.

How do we resist? We fight! We fight the onslaught of negative thoughts. We cast them down. We choose instead to meditate on the Word of God. So many people just forfeit their inheritance because they give in to deceptive thinking that is contrary to the Word of God. You must take authority over those thoughts and break their power.

We resist by refusing to give in to negative emotions. It is very easy to give in to self-pity when things are not going your way. Have you ever seen a soldier who is crying and feeling sorry for himself go into a battle and win? No way! He probably would be strongly reprimanded by his commanding officer. It is not that we are to be unemotional robots. We feel things and experience ups and downs in our emotions. We must not, however, give in to the negative emotions in the middle of the battle, or we may sink down into despair and hopelessness. One thing that will help you resist is to avoid surrounding yourself with people who will cater to your emotions and have a pity party with you. You need some friends who are fighters!

We also resist with our words. Attacks usually carry some word curses. Negative proclamations go forth and open doors to the spirit realm. We slam those doors shut by counteracting them. We open our mouths and tell the enemy, "Satan, I resist you and I bind your lies. I break your power off my life and command you to go!" When you march around your house resisting the devil and speaking the Word, the whole atmosphere will change! Your words will open the gates of glory and usher in the King.

5. Break it by standing firm.

> But none of these things move me, neither count I my life dear unto myself, so that I might finish my course with joy, and the ministry, which I have received of the Lord Jesus, to testify the gospel of the grace of God.
> —ACTS 20:24, KJV

Paul was not moved by the natural things going on around him. Attacks manifest and create storms around us. Satan attacks our finances, makes someone get mad at us, or releases an offense, all with a purpose to move us away from the promise. We must heed the advice of Paul and stay firmly planted.

That is much easier said than done. Often in the middle of the battle your mind and emotions are screaming at you.

You want to retreat. You want to throw in the towel. This is the time when you must stand. You must stand on what God says and refuse to cede an inch of ground.

Standing is the result of spiritual conviction. When you believe something is absolutely true, then you will not budge. Many people are easily moved because they are not deeply rooted and planted. We must strive to develop deep roots in our spirit life and become planted in our purpose. As we journey forward in our destiny, there will be ups and downs, but if we are planted, we will remain faithful.

Sometimes just staying put is a tremendous victory strategy. As you refuse to let the devil push you off your purpose, you conquer his lies. Stand firm in the Word of the Lord. Stand firm in your prayer life. Stand firm in your convictions and rest in the truth that "this too shall pass!"

6. Break it with fasting.

> Is this not the fast that I have chosen: To loose the bonds of wickedness, to undo the heavy burdens, to let the oppressed go free, and that you break every yoke?
> —ISAIAH 58:6, NKJV

Prayer and fasting are power twins. Fasting is the laying aside of food for a set period of time in order to focus entirely on Jesus. There are many different ways to fast. The key is seeking God and discerning which road He is leading you to travel.

Why is fasting an effective tool for breaking an attack? Because it submits one part of your being that is not renewed (your carnal man, your body) to the part of you that is renewed (your spirit man). You set yourself aside for a designated period of time to come into the presence of the Lord. Your intimacy with Him and separation unto Him break bonds, remove burdens, and slice cords. It is not because of the sacrifice you make; it is because of the intimacy you gain with Him. When you fast and pray, you put yourself in a position of spiritual acceleration and heightened awareness.

Many people have opinions on fasting. I don't believe it should ever become a religious work, but it should be a life-giving part of your relationship with God.

Beware of Offense

While you are putting your faith to work and breaking the power of hell as we've studied, be on guard for the force of offense. In a season when you are vulnerable, the enemy would love to bring emotional wounds into your life. Because your emotions are already raw from the onslaught, it is very easy to become offended by things that would normally not even bother you. Offense is sent to ensnare you and block your breakthrough.

One of the best ways to guard against it as you are coming out of a spiritual attack is to conduct a daily heart-check in prayer. Simply come before the Lord and ask Him to search your heart. Tell Him you want to be aware of anything the enemy is trying to plant and use against you:

> Search me, O God, and know my heart: try me, and know my thoughts.
> —Psalm 139:23, kjv

You will be shocked by how swiftly the Holy Spirit moves and reveals things for you to drop. Offense turns into baggage that hinders you and weighs you down. It contaminates your flow and imprisons your mind. It can create an entirely separate level of emotional weight that will confine you.

Just be quick to forgive. If someone hurts you, let it go. As you are breaking the larger spiritual attack off your life, give no room to any other demonic operation. Release the offense, sever the ties, and let it all go!

Use all the tools that we have outlined here to realize your freedom. Make a decision that:

- You will not embrace the evil accusations of the enemy.

- You will not move away from your assignment.

- You will not get stuck in a rut.

- You will not allow the present challenge to determine your future course!

Spiritual attacks will come. Challenges will arise, and the voice of the enemy will speak. The truth is that God's Word outlasts them all:

> As for God, His way has integrity; the word of the LORD is proven; He is a shield to all those who take refuge in Him. For who is God except the LORD? Or who is a rock besides our God? It is God who clothes me with strength, and gives my way integrity. He makes my feet like the feet of a deer, and causes me to stand on my high places. He trains my hands for war, so that my arms bend a bow of bronze. You have given me the shield of Your salvation, and Your right hand has held me up, and Your gentleness has made me great. You have lengthened my stride under me, so that my feet did not slip. I pursued my enemies and overtook them; I did not return until they were destroyed.
>
> —PSALM 18:30–37

His declaration over you and about you is the final authority, and I cannot find any scriptures that authorize your destruction. Our God is a mighty man of war, and He teaches our hands to fight.

Your eyes have been opened to recognize a spiritual attack, and your sword has been sharpened to break it!

NOTES

CHAPTER 1
WHAT IS A SPIRITUAL ATTACK?

1. George Bloomer, *Spiritual Warfare* (New Kensington, PA: Whitaker House, 2004), 157–158.

2. Abarim Publications, "The Name Ziklag in the Bible," accessed April 22, 2016, http://www.abarim-publications.com/Meaning /Ziklag.html#.VxpDmdQrJph.

3. Catherine Mullins, in discussion with the author, February 2015.

CHAPTER 2
DISCERNING AN ATTACK

1. Norvel Hayes, *How to Cast Out Devils* (Tulsa, OK: Harrison House, 2013), 14.

2. *Brown, Driver, Briggs, Gesenius Lexicon*, s.v. "*ro'eh*," Bible StudyTools.com, "The NAS Old Testament Hebrew Lexicon," accessed April 22, 2016, http://www.biblestudytools.com/lexicons /hebrew/nas/roeh.html.

3. *Merriam-Webster Online*, s.v. "revelation," accessed April 22, 2016, http://www.merriam-webster.com/dictionary/revelation.

4. James Strong, *Strong's Exhaustive Concordance of the Bible*, s.v. "*pneuma*," G4151, BlueLetterBible.org, accessed April 25, 2016, https://www.blueletterbible.org/lang/lexicon/lexicon.cfm?Strongs =G4151.

5. Strong, *Strong's Exhaustive Concordance of the Bible*, s.v. "*python*," G4436, BlueLetterBible.org, accessed April 25, 2016, https://www.blueletterbible.org/lang/Lexicon/Lexicon.cfm?strongs =G4436&t=KJV.

Chapter 3

Attack Symptom 1—Lack of Spiritual Passion

1. Lester Sumrall, *Demons: The Answer Book* (New Kensington, PA: Whitaker House, 1993), 154.

Chapter 4

Attack Symptom 2—Extreme Frustration

1. *Merriam-Webster Online*, s.v. "frustration," accessed April 25, 2016, http://www.merriam-webster.com/dictionary/frustration.

2. Bill Johnson, *The Supernatural Power of a Transformed Mind* (Shippensburg, PA: Destiny Image, 2005), 114–115.

Chapter 5

Attack Symptom 3—Confusion About Purpose

1. Myles Munroe, *In Pursuit of Purpose* (Shippensburg, PA: Destiny Image, 1992), 28. Italics in original.

Chapter 6

Attack Symptom 4—Lack of Peace

1. Joyce Meyer, *Let God Fight Your Battles* (New York: Faith-Words, 2015), 111–112.

2. *Merriam-Webster Online*, s.v. "reconcile," accessed April 26, 2016, http://www.merriam-webster.com/dictionary/reconcile.

3. Strong, *Strong's Exhaustive Concordance of the Bible*, s.v. "*nous*," G3563, BlueLetterBible.org, accessed April 26, 2016, https://www.blueletterbible.org/lang/Lexicon/Lexicon.cfm?strongs=G3563&t=KJV.

4. BibleHub.com, "Helps Word-Studies," s.v. "*kardia*," accessed April 26, 2016, http://biblehub.com/greek/2588.htm.

5. *Thayer's and Smith's Bible Dictionary*, as viewed at BibleStudy Tools.com, "The KJV New Testament Greek Lexicon," s.v. "*hupodeo*," G5265, accessed April 26, 2016, http://www.biblestudytools.com/lexicons/greek/kjv/hupodeo.html.

6. *NAS Exhaustive Concordance of the Bible With Hebrew-Aramaic and Greek Dictionaries*, s.v. "*rechoboth*," H7344, viewed at Biblehub.com, accessed April 27, 2016, http://biblehub.com/hebrew/7344.htm.

CHAPTER 7
ATTACK SYMPTOMS—UNUSUALLY SLUGGISH AND TIRED

1. *Oxford Dictionaries Online*, s.v. "curse," accessed April 27, 2016, http://www.oxforddictionaries.com/us/definition/american _english/curse.

CHAPTER 8
ATTACK SYMPTOM 6—STRONG URGE TO QUIT ASSIGNMENT

1. Rebecca Greenwood, "7 Ways to Disarm Strongholds of the Mind," CharismaNews.com, January 1, 2015, accessed April 27, 2016, http://www.charismanews.com/opinion/47830-7-ways-to-disarm -strongholds-of-the-mind.

2. Ibid.

CHAPTER 9
ATTACK SYMPTOM 7—DRAWN BACK TOWARD OLD BONDAGES

1. Neil T. Anderson, *Winning Spiritual Warfare* (Eugene, OR: Harvest House, 1991), 8.

CHAPTER 10
ATTACK SYMPTOM 8—QUESTIONING DIRECTION
AND CALL THAT WAS ONCE CLEAR

1. *Merriam-Webster Online*, s.v. "intimidate," accessed April 28, 2016, http://www.merriam-webster.com/dictionary/intimidate.

2. Sarah Zielinski, "Secrets of a Lion's Roar," Smithsonian.com, November 3, 2011, accessed May 2, 2016, http://www .smithsonianmag.com/science-nature/secrets-of-a-lions-roar -126395997/?no-ist.

3. Leonard Ravenhill, "What Is Your Vision?," sermon, September 14, 1994, Ravenhill.org, accessed May 2, 2016, http://www .ravenhill.org/vision.htm.

4. *Merriam-Webster Online*, s.v. "confused," accessed May 2, 2016, http://www.merriam-webster.com/dictionary/confused.

CHAPTER 11
THE BATTLE OF THE MIND

1. Lisa Bevere, "The Key to Totally Transforming Your Life," CharismaNews.com, November 27, 2014, accessed May 2, 2016, http://www.charismanews.com/opinion/46277-the-key-to-totally -transforming-your-life.

2. Strong, *Strong's Exhaustive Concordance of the Bible*, s.v. "*anakainosis*," G342, BlueLetterBible.org, accessed May 2, 2016, https://www.blueletterbible.org/lang/Lexicon/Lexicon.cfm?strongs =G342&t=KJV.

3. See Strong, *Strong's Exhaustive Concordance of the Bible*, s.v. "*kardia*," G2588, BlueLetterBible.org, accessed May 2, 2016, https://www.blueletterbible.org/lang/Lexicon/Lexicon.cfm?strongs =G2588&t=KJV.

4. Strong, *Strong's Exhaustive Concordance of the Bible*, s.v. "*mak'ob*," H4341, BlueLetterBible.org, accessed May 2, 2016, https://www.blueletterbible.org/lang/Lexicon/Lexicon.cfm?strongs =H4341&t=KJV.

Chapter 12
Three Types of Common Attacks

1. See Strong, *Strong's Exhaustive Concordance of the Bible*, s.v. "*kairos*," G2540, BlueLetterBible.org, accessed May 2, 2016, https://www.blueletterbible.org/lang/Lexicon/Lexicon.cfm?strongs =G2540&t=KJV.

Chapter 13
Freedom From Attacks!

1. *Merriam-Webster Online*, s.v. "resist," accessed May 3, 2016, http://www.merriam-webster.com/dictionary/resist.

Ryan LeStrange Ministries is circling the globe with fire! Ryan has an apostolic mandate to spark and fan the flame of revival, unleash the power of God, and ignite revival hubs in cities and regions around the earth. Ryan delivers a strong message of faith and deliverance with revelatory truths on the apostolic and prophetic ministries. He is cofounder of *awakeningtv.com* and the New Breed Revival Network, both of which carry the message of revival. He has authored several books, including *The Fire of Revival, Releasing the Prophetic,* and *Revival Hubs Rising* (coauthored with Jennifer LeClaire) and offers numerous audio series to those seeking and longing for *revival* and *awakening* in this hour.

Invite Ryan
@ ryanlestrange.com

CONNECT with Ryan:
www.periscope.tv/RyanLeStrange
twitter.com/RyanLeStrange
www.facebook.com/ryanlestrangeministries
youtube.com/user/TheRyanLeStrange

Ryan LeStrange Ministries
P.O. Box 16206
Bristol, VA 24209

CONNECT WITH US!

CHARISMA
HOUSE

(Spiritual Growth)

f Facebook.com/CharismaHouse

𝕐 @CharismaHouse

◎ Instagram.com/CharismaHouseBooks

(Health)

𝓟 Pinterest.com/CharismaHouse

REALMS
(Fiction)

f Facebook.com/RealmsFiction